Customs and Practices
of the
Moravian Church

Adelaide L. Fries

Revised Edition 2003

Customs and Practices of the Moravian Church

Copyright © 2003
Interprovincial Board of Communication
Moravian Church in North America
PO Box 1245
Bethlehem, PA 18016-1245
800.732.0591
www.moravian.org
All rights reserved.

Book design: Sandy Fay,
Laughing Horse Graphics, Doylestown, PA
ISBN: 1-878422-76-6

Printed in the United States of America
Second printing, 2009

PREFACES

I. A PIONEER CHURCH

II. A LITURGICAL CHURCH

III. THE CHURCH YEAR

IV. A CHURCH THAT REMEMBERS

V. A CHURCH FAMILY

Dr. Adelaide L. Fries is the archivist of the Southern Province of the Moravian Church in America. She has written this book at the request of the widely distributed "Know Your Church" publications undertaken by the [Interprovincial] Board [of Christian Education].

Dr. Fries was born in Winston-Salem in a Moravian family which traces its ancestry back to Zinzendorf, the father of the renewed Church. Early in life she displayed an interest in historical matters. She was educated at Salem Academy and College, undertook research in the Moravian Archives, Bethlehem, Pennsylvania, and Herrnhut, Germany, and for many years has studied appreciatively in the Archives of the Southern Province. Three honorary degrees, in each case the degree being Doctor of Letters, have been bestowed upon her by Moravian College, Wake Forest, and the University of North Carolina in recognition of her efforts. Her usefulness as a historian is evidenced by her popularity as a speaker and writer. Among her works are *Records of the Moravians in North Carolina* and the popular *Road to Salem.* She is the co-author of the centennial history, *Forsyth, a County on the March.*

All points of this present volume have been carefully checked in the historical records of our Church and with many informed persons. It is our hope that this book may serve as a source of information and interest on matters pertaining to the customs and practices of our beloved Church.

The enthusiastic reception given *Customs and Practices of the Moravian Church* has merited a republication of Dr. Adelaide L. Fries' book.

This edition, prepared by the Commission on Publications of the Southern Province's Board of Christian Education and Evangelism, is presented with revisions which include recent developments in the organizational structure of the Church enacted by the General Synod of 1957.

Dr. Fries' death, in 1949, concluded a life of devoted service to her Church. This volume is offered as a tribute to her life-long interest in the Moravian heritage and the valuable contribution her influence continues to make toward a deeper appreciation of the Church's life and witness.

THE COMMISSION ON PUBLICATIONS
THE BOARD OF CHRISTIAN EDUCATION AND
EVANGELISM, SOUTH

Raymond E. Ebert	R. Gordon Spaugh
George G. Higgins	Edwin L. Stockton
Burton J. Rights	F. Herbert Weber

This is a book about "containers" — the containers of the faith of the early Moravian Church. It is about the customs and practices which contained their love for the living Christ.

If we are interested only in the containers and ignore the contents, we will be caught "holding the bag," an empty bag. Revering the containers can be a kind of idolatry, too. It is the contents that are important.

As you read about the containers, look for the contents. Be aware of these people's experiences with God the Father and the Holy Spirit and with Jesus, their Elder Brother and Savior. Be also aware of their experiences with one another and in serving their Master.

After reading this book, give some thought and effort to your church forming some new customs and practices to contain your experiences of the love of Jesus for you and your love for Him. Ask the living Christ to lead you into new fields of service for Him.

Your own faith and love for the living Christ will produce new containers, and there will be new customs and practices in the Moravian Church.

This edition has been given a new cover and some corrections were made by the Committee: the brethren F. Herbert Weber, C. Bruce Weber, Bill Glance, Robert Iobst, William McElveen and the sisters Patricia Johnson and Lucile Newman (cover design). Brother George Higgins also gave much help.

It was asked, when work began on this edition of *Customs and Practices,* whether it would be an updating or a rewriting. The answer is yes.

Much of what Miss Adelaide wrote is as timeless as the Moravian Church itself. There will always be lovefeasts in many churches and not in some of them, for example. But much has transpired since the first edition was published in 1949. Changes have occurred not only in the Moravian Church but in the Christian Church at large. Among Moravians, for example, we have had two hymnals published since then, each with its own unique contributions and idiosyncrasies.

In the Christian Church at large, the New Revised Standard Version has propelled the Bible into modern terms, whether for good or ill. Spanning a number of denominations is the three-year lectionary, a development of the 1980's that has altered much of the Scriptural emphasis in the cycle of the church year. Moreover, Euro-American Christians (and Moravians) have opened their eyes to the much larger world of Christian faith that literally spans the globe.

From the standpoint of those and other breathtaking changes, this edition of Miss Adelaide's *Customs and Practices* has been updated.

In addition, much of what Miss Adelaide wrote has of necessity undergone careful rewriting. In a word, her style was born of a more formal era, and we suspect too that her writing was influenced by her German heritage. Many sentences cried out for simplification, and we have done so, we hope without losing Miss Adelaide's intent, or perhaps even reinforcing it.

Such has been our aim — updating, yes, rewriting, yes, but customs and practices that Miss Adelaide knew, that her Moravian ancestors knew, that we know today, all one and the same and all pointing to our Chief Elder of the Church, Christ Jesus.

C. Daniel Crews, Archivist
Moravian Archives
Winston-Salem, North Carolina

Richard W. Starbuck, Assistant Archivist
Moravian Archives
Winston-Salem, North Carolina

January, 2003

chapter 1

A PIONEER CHURCH

Standard Bearer of Protestantism

History assigns to the Moravian Church the position of "Standard Bearer of Protestantism." With the exception of certain pre-Reformation groups that were not really classified as churches, it is in point of time the oldest of the Protestant churches.

The records show that those who composed its first membership were the forerunners of the movement known as the Reformation. They were followers of the great pre-Reformation preacher, educator, and martyr, John Hus of Bohemia, who was burned at the stake in Constance, Germany, in 1415, one hundred and two years before Martin Luther began the movement in Germany which developed into the Reformation, and which also produced Erasmus and Calvin to carry the Reformation into other parts of Europe.

John Hus was burned at the stake because he refused to give up his belief that the doctrines set forth in the Bible should be followed by Christians. His view that the authority of the Scriptures took precedence over the authority of the Church brought him into conflict with the Roman Catholic Church of his day.

But though the church and civil rulers of that day killed Hus they could not destroy his teachings. He had been a much beloved preacher, and there were many who remembered what he had said and what he had written. For 16 years his followers, through what are known as the Hussite Wars, tried to establish his doctrines by force of arms, but they gained only one point, the right to give the Cup to the congregation in the holy communion.

When the Hussite Wars ended, people began to ask themselves whether there might not be a better way to carry out their purpose. A group withdrew from Prague to the estate of Litice (Lititz), on the border of Bohemia, where they planned to live Christian lives according to the Bible, as Hus had explained it. That was in 1457. Ten years later they found it necessary to establish their own independent ministry. So the Unitas Fratrum, the Unity of Brethren, was firmly established 60 years before the Protestant Reformation began.

"The Pioneer Church of Christian Missions" is another designation which is generally accorded to the Moravian Church. The beginning of Moravian missions was in 1732, which is 60 years before the mission movement started in England under William Carey, and 78 years before the organization of the American Board of Commissioners for Foreign Missions. Before 1732 there had been a few brave members of other churches who had attempted to go to non-Christians, but the Moravians were the first Protestants to undertake missions as a church enterprise.

While not the first Protestant church to come to America, the Moravian Church came in colonial days. There was a temporary settlement in Georgia from 1735 to 1740, and permanent settlements began in Pennsylvania in 1740 and in North Carolina in 1753.

In 1749 the Parliament of Great Britain gave formal recognition to the Moravian Church as an "ancient Protestant Episcopal Church." This act of Parliament made permanent the name of the renewed Unitas Fratrum as the "Moravian Church," a name already current at some places because in 1722 men, women, and children, descendants of the ancient Unitas Fratrum, came from the province of Moravia into what is now Saxony in Germany, seeking religious liberty.

The name "Moravian Church" soon ceased to have any national significance, for the Unitas Fratrum grew rapidly by the accession of members from many of the European states and from other denominations. Comparatively few of the settlers in Moravian centers in America were born in Moravia or were descended from those born in Moravia, but they had inherited the history of the Church and the name was so generally and appropriately used that it has been accepted as one of the legal names of the Church along with the earlier, Unitas Fratrum, and its English translation, Unity of Brethren.

Strictly speaking, therefore, the name Moravian Church emphasizes its position among the churches as a pioneer church, a Protestant church, an episcopal church (i.e., a church with bishops), and a church of recognized standing in America from colonial days to the present. The name Unitas Fratrum stresses the doctrine of Christian fellowship under Jesus Christ, regardless of the race or the denomination from which a member has come.

Today the Moravian Church consists of 19 provinces that are found in many areas of the world and among many peoples. As the constitution of the Unitas Fratrum states, "Some are found in highly industrialized communities; others are in developing regions of the earth. As a consequence, the Provinces of the Unity offer a wide variety of economic, social and political development."

Because of this divergence some of the younger provinces, as the constitution continues,

> *must of necessity look to other Provinces or to the Unity as a whole for assistance with workers and money and for encouragement and advice. Such Provinces are considered to be in affiliation*

with the supporting Province. This support is given and received in a spirit of mutual love and concern and is an essential feature of the brotherhood of the Unitas Fratrum.

In regard to the denominational lines it may be noted that in 1741 Henry Antes, a member of the Reformed Church in Pennsylvania, and Nicholas Ludwig (Count Zinzendorf), a bishop of the Moravian Church, tried to develop friendship and cooperation among the numerous denominations in Pennsylvania. The attempt failed because of jealousies and misunderstandings, but today various efforts are being made to secure cooperation among Christian churches which failed 250 years ago. One such effort brought full communion with the Evangelical Lutheran Church in 2000. Currently (2003) the Moravian Church is in dialog with the Episcopal Church and with members of the Reformed tradition.

In the minutes of a "synodical conference" held in England in 1750 there is an interesting statement of the relation of the Moravian Church to other churches of that day. For instance, a kindly feeling toward the Eastern Orthodox Church was advised "because it brought us the Gospel," when the Greek priests, Cyril and Methodius, went as missionaries to heathen Moravia in A.D. 863. Of the Roman Catholic Church "we must not speak ill," because "we were once of their household," although "they have bidden us farewell." "The English Church has stood by us as long as it existed. They think we can help them and all Christendom." "We have particular connections with the Lutherans, many of whom have joined the Unity."

Today the Moravian Church occupies a middle position between those churches which insist on the Apostolic Succession for the consecration of their bishops and those newer denominations which have established their own forms of ordination. The words of Bishop Edward Rondthaler sum up the position of the Moravian Church among the churches:

Because of formal recognition of our Episcopate by act of the British Parliament in 1749, the Episcopal Church has fraternized with us for nearly two centuries and has welcomed our bishops to her pulpits.

Calvin and his fellow reformers at Geneva were warm friends of the Unity, and the synodical character of our Church has, among Presbyterians, confirmed this old attachment.

With Luther our forefathers were in friendly correspondence, and learned much from him, and we have always declared our substantial agreement with the Confession of Augsburg.

With the Methodists we have the tender tie of the conversion of the Wesleys through their converse with Boehler, Spangenberg, and others. Thus we are united in the special emphasis which we and they are accustomed to lay on the experience of the forgiveness of sins through faith in our sin-atoning Saviour.

And although we baptize infants, and administer baptism by sprinkling or pouring, yet our kindly appreciation of the Baptist position, and that close adherence to the Scriptures which we prize in common with them, has been the occasion of much fellowship between us.

Government of the Moravian Church

From the beginning the Moravian Church has had leaders of vision, leaders with ideals and ideas far in advance of their own era.

In 1457 there was no democratic government in church or state. Priests and potentates ruled their people with an iron hand.

In spite of this custom the followers of Hus who gathered in the little village of Kunvald on the estate of Litice in Bohemia organized on strictly democratic principles. Members elected the elders, and such other boards and officials as were needed for the supervision of their congregation and village. Women as well as men were chosen for office.

As the movement spread and other congregations were organized, contact was maintained through conferences and through synods to which the congregations sent elected delegates. They sought to make effective the words of Jesus: One is your Master, even Christ; and all ye are brethren (Matt. 23:8, KJV).

All important matters came up for consideration by these synods. They adopted rules and regulations; they formulated doctrines; they outlined policies in times of peace and in times of persecution. A synod decided that an independent ministry had become necessary; a synod elected the men who should receive ordination as the first priests and bishops from among the "Brethren." Throughout the period of the ancient Unitas Fratrum (1457 to 1650's), the synod was the supreme authority among the congregations of the Church, which gradually spread from Bohemia into the adjacent countries of Moravia and Poland.

In the Counter-Reformation which followed the death of Martin Luther, the Protestant cause in Germany was saved by Gustavus Adolphus of Sweden, but the army which the Unitas Fratrum, the Reformed, and the Lutheran Churches put into the field in Bohemia and Moravia was utterly defeated by the Catholic forces. Thousands of the best citizens of those countries were driven into exile or were executed in Prague on June 21, 1621, giving rise to the name "Day of Blood." After a time formal organization ceased in the Unity of Brethren.

When the emigrants from Moravia re-organized the Unitas Fratrum in Herrnhut, Saxony, in the 1720's, they retained the forms which had been so effective earlier. Again men and women were elected to office by vote of the members; boards and committees served under rules and regulations which the members adopted. Again synods took a leading place in the church polity.

The same is true in America and Canada today. Each Moravian congregation holds an annual church council, in which members of the congregation elect officers and boards and transact such other business as may be necessary. The Southern Province has a Florida District for its churches there. The Northern Province, being continent-wide, for convenience in administration has Eastern, Western, and Canadian Districts as well as the provincial structure.

Provincial synods are held at intervals established by the rules of each province. In those synods lay and ministerial delegates receive reports on the past intersynodal period and set courses of action for the next intersynodal period. To oversee such action, synods elect a Provincial Elders' Conference (PEC) and members of other provincial boards.

Delegates from the provinces meet in a Unity Synod scheduled since 1967 to be held at intervals of every seven years. During the 18th century the General Synod (as it was then known) had authority over many interests of the individual provinces. During the 19th century the provinces became independent; but the General Synod still had executive control over the missions of the Moravian Church, which between synods were managed by an interprovincial committee sitting in Herrnhut. After World War I it was necessary to reorganize the mission work and to commit the various mission fields to individual provinces for supervision. To Unity Synod is left the important task of maintaining supervision of the doctrines of the Moravian Church and of furthering its worldwide fellowship.

By action of the Unity Synod of 1967 the affairs of the Unitas Fratrum are managed between synods by a Unity Board which consists of one member from each province "governed by a Synod." The Unity Board normally carries on its business by correspondence but may meet in emergencies. One of its duties is to call the Unity Synod and "decide on the place and date of convening."

The Ministry of the Moravian Church

When the group of followers of John Hus gathered in the village of Kunvald in Bohemia in 1457, they had no intention of separating themselves from the established church. They thought that it would be possible for them to live quiet, simple, Christian lives, served by priests of the Catholic or of the Utraquist Church who were in sympathy with their purpose. For many years the Waldenses, followers of Peter Waldo of France, had been such a group within the Catholic Church, so the plan of the Hussites seemed plausible enough.

Unexpected growth drew persecution, which inspired further growth, not only at Kunvald but also in the surrounding region. By 1467 there were not enough priests to serve them all, and this finally forced them to establish their own ministry.

At that time no ordination was considered valid unless it was received at the hands of a bishop who was in the so-called Apostolic Succession, that is, in a direct line of succession from the Apostles. The question was where to find a bishop who would be able and willing to give them this type of consecration, and so place the ordination of their ministers beyond the criticism of their enemies. They thought to have the Waldensians' Bishop Stephen consecrate one of three priests who were willing to accept episcopal consecration, but Stephen had been arrested by Catholic authorities and burned at the stake. Consequently they turned to another Waldensian priest who was "just as old as Stephen and venerable in the tradition." This laying on of hands, the Brethren viewed as "validly confirmed through the Supreme Bishop," Christ Jesus; and one of their priests "received consecration as a Bishop at the hands of an old Waldensian." Thus for all intents and purposes, the

Apostolic Succession had been passed on to the Unitas Fratrum.

The defeat of the Protestant forces in Bohemia in 1621 and the wholesale persecution which followed, threatened the Unitas Fratrum with extinction, but Bishop John Amos Comenius and the other bishops of that day carefully preserved the episcopate, consecrating younger priests so that the succession might be assured in case the Unity was revived.

When such a revival took place in Herrnhut in the 1720's two bishops of the ancient Unitas Fratrum were still living, Daniel Jablonsky of Berlin and Christian Sitkovius of Poland. Bishop Jablonsky, with the approval of Bishop Sitkovius, consecrated David Nitschmann (called the "carpenter" to distinguish him from other men of the same name). Thus the Moravian episcopacy dating from 1467 has continued to the present day.

Moravian bishops hold no executive position by virtue of their office. Their function is primarily to ordain men and women into the ministry, and bishops consecrated in one province hold their episcopal standing throughout all the other provinces of the Unity, and for life. Custom recognizes them as "pastors of the pastors." Moravian bishops may serve as pastors of congregations, or election may place them in executive positions. Bishops are elected from among the presbyters of the Moravian Church.

Elevation to the rank of presbyter is authorized by a Provincial Elders' Conference for deacons of the Moravian Church, in recognition of faithful and approved service in the ministry. Consecration as a presbyter is given by a bishop. It confers no added privilege to those held as a deacon.

Those who have completed a theological course and are considered suitable candidates for the ministry are ordained as deacons by a bishop before being placed in charge of a congregation or called to other service. Occasionally lay workers are ordained after they have received special training under the direction of a Provincial Elders' Conference and are serving as full-time supply pastors of congregations.

Deacons in the Moravian Church are considered fully ordained. They may administer the sacrament of the Lord's Supper, baptize infants or adults, administer the rite of confirmation, and perform the marriage ceremony.

Ministers transferring from another denomination to the Moravian Church are accepted as deacons. They can become presbyters only through consecration by a Moravian bishop.

The Unity Synod of 1967 established the office of acolytes for lay servants who exercise a "particular responsibility in the Congregation or Province." The duties may include "assisting the pastor in pastoral duties" and "assisting in serving the elements of the Holy Communion...." Acolytes, or Acolouths as the German word, may be elected by the Boards of Elders and Trustees of a congregation, but their reception must be authorized by the Provincial Elders' Conference. The office applies only in the congregation making the selection and is not transferable if the acolyte moves to another congregation.

The Moravian Church Seal and Motto

The seal of the Moravian Church was first used by bishops going back to the 16th century certainly and probably to the time when the episcopate was secured by the Unity in the 15th century. The seal was transferred to the bishops of the renewed Unitas Fratrum, or Moravian Church, when David Nitschmann received episcopal consecration from the bishops of the ancient Unity, Jablonsky and Sitkovius.

In the center of the seal is an *Agnus Dei* (Lamb of God), a favorite symbol of Christ in the early Christian Church (John 1:29; Rev. 5:5; etc.). It is the figure of a lamb holding a staff with a cross at the top. From the staff hangs the banner of victory, and on the banner is another cross. Around the Moravian seal is the inscription, *Vicit agnus noster, eum Sequamur,* "Our

Lamb has conquered, let us follow Him."

Moravians are quick to quote a "motto," and since we have been doing so for the last century or so we can call it a custom. The motto is, "In essentials, unity; in nonessentials, liberty; in all things, love."

Variously attributed to St. Augustine of Hippo and more frequently to Peter Meiderlin, a 16th century Lutheran theologian, the phrase also appears in the last published work of the Moravian bishop John Amos Comenius entitled *The One Thing Needful*. After a lapse of a couple of centuries the motto began to appear within the Moravian Church in the mid-1800's, and by 1900 had appeared in the Southern Province's newspaper, *The Wachovia Moravian*.

All-embracing as the motto seems, it must be remembered that Comenius used it in the context of Christian faith, not as a proclamation of "anything goes" or "everybody else must give way to what I want to do." Certainly the motto is, as Comenius understood it, a sublime statement of Christian forbearance, acceptance, and love.

"The Ground of the Unity"

The Moravian motto invites the question, "What are essentials?" "Essentials," one would think, can be found enumerated in a church's doctrinal creed. Yet such Moravian luminaries as Bishop Edward Rondthaler and Harry E. Stocker have pointed out that rather than a strictly formulated creed, the Moravian Church remains broadly evangelical with "Christ and Him crucified" (1 Cor. 2:2) as our "point of view." Thus, while the creeds of the early Church, the Nicene and Apostles' Creeds, "formulate the prime articles of faith found in the Scriptures," as Br. Stocker put it, "every doctrine and every practice is considered by the Moravians in its bearing upon the atonement, the love, the living presence of the Christ of God," as Br.

Rondthaler wrote. For every doctrinal statement is of human origin, and consequently is doomed in its attempt to encompass the Living God for all time. Along with the Nicene Creed (it appears on page 22 of the 1995 *Moravian Book of Worship*) and the Apostles' Creed (on pages 3, 166, and 170), the worldwide Moravian Church in various regions accepts creeds of other churches — the Small Catechism of the Lutheran Church, for example, or the Thirty-Nine Articles of the Church of England — as giving clear expression of Christian faith.

In the ancient Unity, doctrinal statements were formulated primarily in response to inquiries of other churches. For itself the Unity relied on the essentials of the gracious good will of God the Father for our salvation, the meritorious saving work of Christ, and the gifts of the Holy Spirit with the essentials of our human response through God's grace of faith, love, and hope. These essentials find expression today in the 1995 *Book of Worship*, pages 52-53.

In the renewed Moravian Church the ruling General Synod over the years formulated various "essential points" of Christian doctrine. At first only four in number in the 1700's, these points grew until by 1900 there were eight. But formulating a list of "essential features" of doctrine runs the danger that they will be declared "eight essentials" of faith and that they will be viewed as a checklist to determine who is a "good" Moravian and who isn't. So finally in 1957, following the devastation of World War II, General Synod retired the listing of doctrinal "points," and adopted a broad doctrinal statement entitled *The Ground of the Unity*. In plain, everyday prose *The Ground of the Unity* proclaims our life in Christ, and it stands today, with slight alterations by succeeding Unity (General) Synods, as our official statement of Moravian doctrine.

Some may see our life in Christ as "do nothing" Christianity. Not so as evidenced throughout the history of the Moravian Church. From its outset in the 1450's the ancient Unity sought not to formulate a separate doctrinal creed, but rather a practical daily life in Christ, or as Br. Rondthaler put it, a "union of believers in Christian *living*" (Br. Rondthaler's emphasis). This Christian living has found its greatest expression in missions, to which we now turn.

Moravian Missions

The ancient Unitas Fratrum carried out much home mission work but nothing along the line of foreign missions. When dates and maps are considered, this was natural. Europe was just awakening to the age of discovery. Explorers began opening new lands; adventurers set out seeking gold; a few colonists made their way to the New World. Occasionally a wandering priest baptized natives who met the Europeans, but permanent work for Christ was lacking.

When Columbus was discovering America the Unitas Fratrum was prospering under its second great leader, Bishop Luke of Prague. One year after the Pilgrims landed at Plymouth Rock in 1620 the ancient Unitas Fratrum was overwhelmed in the Counter-Reformation. The century that followed was one of reaction, coldness, and formalism, and the Unitas Fratrum existed only as a "hidden seed" with its episcopate carefully guarded by Bishop John Amos Comenius.

Finally there was a rebirth of Christian warmth in the Pietistic movement in Germany, and it furnished the atmosphere in which little Nicholas Ludwig (Count Zinzendorf), received his religious training.

His father died when Zinzendorf was but an infant. When his mother married again and moved with her husband to the court at Berlin, she left the child with his grandmother, Countess von Gersdorf. The Countess was an ardent Pietist, and through her the boy was led into a warm Christian life at an early age.

When he was in the boarding school at Halle he learned of the peoples in far-off lands, and his tender heart was touched by thoughts of their great need. With three companions of his own age he formed a little club, which they called the "Order of the Mustard Seed." The boys knew they belonged to the nobility and when they became of age they would have money and influence, so they covenanted together that when they were old enough they would either take or send the Gospel to the world — the tiny mustard seed of desire should become a tree of attainment.

Unlike the majority of such boyish plans this one reached fulfillment. The "Order" continued with their growth, spreading to include notable men of like mind and purpose. Cardinal Noailles of France was a member; so was President Reichenbach of Berlin; as was Archbishop Potter of Canterbury, England. With his remarkable nature of democracy Count Zinzendorf shared his thoughts of the non-Christian world with such notables on the one hand and with his Moravian tenants on the other. Among the latter he found people who were willing, even eager, to carry the message to the ends of the earth.

In the year 1731 the Count visited the court of Denmark, in Copenhagen, where he was received with great honor. He attended a coronation, and the king himself decorated him with the jewel of the Order of the Dannebrog.

Of more lasting importance was his meeting with two Inuit men from Greenland and an African from the Danish West Indies, from whom he heard much of conditions in those countries. He became aroused anew for foreign missions, wishing to send help to Hans Egede, a Dane who had been laboring single-handed and without success in Greenland, and to the African slaves in the West Indies.

Returning to Herrnhut he told the congregation what he had seen and heard, and immediately volunteers for both fields came forward. Months of instruction followed, and on August 21, 1732, Leonard Dober and David Nitschmann set out for St. Thomas in the West Indies.

The African, Anton, had warned the congregation of

Herrnhut that the missionaries would probably have to sell themselves as slaves in order to reach the slaves of the island. This did not come to pass, for the two men secured the needed permission without that tremendous sacrifice. But during the following years, when other missionaries came and the work spread to other islands, many lives were lost because of the climate and a manner of living to which they were not accustomed. Undeterred, the work continued and today there are strong Moravian congregations on the eight islands of the Eastern West Indies Province.

On January 19, 1733, Matthaeus Stach and two companions left for Greenland. On their arrival things looked unpromising enough. Stach wrote of it:

> *Along the shore were stones,*
> *And here and there some bones*
> *But not a man in sight.*
> *We wandered, brothers three,*
> *In deep perplexity;*
> *At midnight dawned the light.*

As cold and hard as the stones of their coast seemed the hearts of the Inuit, but the missionaries persevered and six years later, Easter Sunday, 1739, Stach was able to baptize their first believers. In the course of time the whole of Greenland was brought to Christ, and finally the Moravian Church turned over its congregations to the Danish Church, which was in a better position to care for them. Greenland had become a Danish home mission rather than a foreign mission, so the Moravian Mission Board called its workers to other fields.

Equally heroic is the story of Africa. In the latter part of the 17th century two missionaries of the Danish-Halle Mission stopped at Cape Town, South Africa, and sent home accounts of the deplorable condition of the natives. For the next 40 years occasional futile attempts were made to arouse interest in Germany. Finally, in 1736, two leaders in the religious life of

Holland sent a call to Herrnhut, asking the Moravians to take up the work, and George Schmidt volunteered, although he had recently returned from six years of imprisonment in Bohemia, where he had gone to preach the Gospel.

On March 11, 1737, Schmidt sailed from Holland and after a voyage of four months he reached Cape Town, desiring "to teach the Hottentots to work and to acquaint them with the Saviour." Unable to speak the language of the natives, he made friends with the first group by joining them after their day's work had ended; sitting with them on the ground, he gave them tobacco and smoked with them.

Going inland to the Vale of Baboons he persevered and after five years he baptized the first believers. But this small success infuriated the white settlers, who wanted the natives to remain ignorant slaves, and two years later they forced Schmidt to return to Europe. He died in 1785 while kneeling in prayer, and his friends believed that he died praying for Africa.

Work in South Africa was resumed by the Moravians in 1792. Today there are five Moravian provinces on the continent: South Africa, uniting in 1977 the west district, begun in 1737 and renewed in 1792, and the east district, started in 1828; Tanzania (Southern), 1891; Tanzania (Western), 1897; Tanzania (South-West), 1978; and Tanzania (Rukwa), 1986.

Meanwhile, Moravian missionaries continued to go to the far ends of the earth. Some attempts had only temporary results, but more permanent fields are still active today. Suriname, formerly Dutch Guiana, on the north coast of South America, was begun in 1735; and the adjoining field of Demerara (now known as Guyana), was begun in 1738. In connection with the initial effort at foreign missions on the island of St. Thomas, Moravian missionaries were invited to come to the island of Jamaica in 1754. Unable to enter the closed land of Tibet, Moravian missionaries settled just across the border in northern India in 1856. Work in Labrador commenced in 1771, in Nicaragua in 1849, in Alaska in 1885, in Honduras in 1930, and in Costa Rica in 1980. Most recently, opportunities have arisen in eastern Asia and among the Indians of Mexico.

Prior to World War I these widely scattered mission fields were under the care of an international mission board, sitting at Herrnhut, Saxony. The General Synod of 1931 divided the supervision among the various "home" provinces, though the work remained an interest of the entire Moravian Church. Since the General Synod of 1957 a number of these mission fields have achieved provincial status so that as of 2003 the worldwide Unity consists of 19 provinces.

In addition to the work referred to above, mention should be made of three enterprises that are called "undertakings of the Unity."

The first is the work among the Tibetan refugees at Rajpur in Northern India. This includes a boarding school and hostel and small clinic. Until the Unity Synod of 1967 the Moravian work in Ladakh had been called a province. Political situations in recent years so changed the picture that the humanitarian efforts have replaced the former efforts to carry on congregational work in that part of the world.

The second service of the Moravian Church began among lepers of Palestine. From 1867 to 1951 the Jesus Help Home for lepers was operated near Jerusalem. After the state of Israel was founded the home was closed and the property was sold. A new, modern leprosarium opened its doors at Star Mountain near Ramallah in 1960, and many former patients of the Jesus Help Home came to the new facility. As modern medicine began to treat leprosy effectively, Star Mountain shifted its focus to work with handicapped Arab girls. Despite periodic upheavals in this war-torn land, the work at Star Mountain remains a project supported by all the provinces of the Moravian Unity.

A third work of the Moravian Church is an ecumenical group in the Dominican Republic called the Evangelical Protestant Church. The Board of World Mission of the Moravian Church in North America is one of the co-sponsors of this federation.

Missionary Societies

In the early days of Herrnhut foreign missions were considered a project of the Unity as a whole, and no special missionary societies were organized, although missionaries were sent into many lands.

In April 1741, August Gottlieb Spangenberg organized in London, England, a Society for the Furtherance of the Gospel among the Heathen, which for about 12 years did valuable work in promoting home and foreign missions. This society was revived by its founder in 1776 and became a vital factor in the promotion and management of Moravian missions. It was incorporated in 1921.

The London Association in Aid of Moravian Missions was founded in 1817. Its membership consists largely of non-Moravians, and it contributes annually considerable sums of money in support of Moravian missions.

In Bethlehem, Pennsylvania, a Society for the Furtherance of the Gospel was organized in 1745. This was succeeded in 1787 by the Society for the Propagation of the Gospel among the Heathen, generally spoken of as the SPG, which was incorporated in 1788, and became the leading missionary society in the American Moravian Church. Beginning with 1921 it was the "sending society" for missionaries to Alaska, Nicaragua, and to the Indians in California.

Members of the SPG in North Carolina felt that they were too far away to derive much benefit from the Bethlehem society, so in June 1823 they organized their own Society for the Furtherance of the Gospel, which ultimately ceased to exist. This was followed by a Home Mission Society, which for many years sponsored mission work in the Blue Ridge mountains. The Mount Bethel, Willow Hill, and Crooked Oak congregations are lasting memorials to that work.

Still later there was a Young Men's Missionary Society in Salem, and members of this society, grown to mature years, planned the organization of the Foreign Missionary Society of the Moravian Church, South, which was incorporated in November 1922. Renamed the Mission Society of the Moravian Church, South, in 1975, it is a provincial agency, and its annual lovefeast and business session is attended from all over the Southern Province.

In March 1818 more than 50 women met in Bethlehem, Pennsylvania, and organized their own missionary society. Over the years it bore various names, but ultimately it became known as the Women's Missionary Society. It was probably the oldest missionary society for women in the United States when in the 1980's it joined with other organizations to form the Northeast Pennsylvania Moravian Mission Society. One of Women's Missionary Society's earliest undertakings was to put in print, for the use of the mission, the harmony of the Gospels that had been translated into the Delaware language by David Zeisberger, the veteran missionary to the Indians.

A missionary society for home and foreign missions was organized among the women of Salem, North Carolina, in 1822. This Women's Missionary Society was active for almost 170 years as one of the missionary organizations of Home Moravian Church. Many Southern Province congregations now have their own missionary chapters which are associated in the work of the Mission Society of the Moravian Church, South.

In 1949 an interprovincial Board of Foreign Missions was organized to assume supervision of all missionary work undertaken by the two North American Moravian provinces. It assists the provinces of Alaska, Nicaragua, Honduras, Eastern West Indies, and Guyana. By action of the General Synod of 1957 work among the Indians in California was changed from mission field status to part of the developing California (now Western) District of the Northern Province. Like the Southern Province's Mission Society, in 1975 the Board of Foreign Missions was renamed the Board of World Mission to reflect the wider understanding of mission in the modern world.

With the creation of the interprovincial mission board, the Society for the Propagation of the Gospel in Bethlehem, Pennsylvania, ceased to be the "sending society" for the Moravian provinces in North America. It now, along with the Mission Society in the Southern Province, directs its efforts at promoting interest in missions and in providing funds for missions. These funds are turned over to the Board of World Mission to be disbursed.

The Why of Moravian Mission Today

Given the pluralistic, multicultural world we live in today, some may ask why we bother with the burden of mission work. Quite simply it is because Christ Himself commanded, "Go therefore and make disciples of all nations. . ." (Matt. 27:19). Moreover, the good news we have to share inspires us to our task: That Jesus Christ died upon the cross not just for our sins, but for the salvation of all peoples. It is the incarnate God, the "Christ of God," to use Bishop Edward Rondthaler's term, who has done this marvelous thing, and it is only through Him that we are drawn to Him (see John 12:32).

Thus our burden may seem impossible, since we cannot possibly reach everyone (we must leave some things up to God), but our burden is also very light and joyous as we bring news of salvation to the world.

Such joyous news to convey makes us very truly, as another bishop of the Moravian Church, D. Wayne Burkette, once put it in a memorable sermon, "God's Salt & Light Co." (see Matt. 5:13-16), as we reflect Christ's light in the world so that others may see and rejoice too in their salvation.

Pioneers in Education

John Hus, the "father of the Unitas Fratrum," was a man of comprehensive learning and a master of arts from the University of Prague, which in his day, next to the University of Paris, was the most distinguished seat of learning on the continent of Europe. He served as dean of the philosophical faculty and was twice elected rector of the university. The value which Hus placed on education has remained a distinguishing characteristic of the Moravian Church.

Gregory, under whom the actual founding of the Unitas Fratrum took place, received the education given to candidates for the priesthood. He did not consider himself a learned man and probably took little interest in schools.

His successor, Luke of Prague, consecrated a bishop of the Unitas Fratrum in 1500, held the degree of bachelor of arts from the University of Prague. During the period in which he shaped the course of the Unitas Fratrum, he gave to its worship more form and dignity than it had under Gregory, and he developed the liturgical part of its service. It was a day in which there was no general system of education, but under the leadership of Bishop Luke the Unitas Fratrum established schools in its congregations.

When the printing press was invented the Unitas Fratrum bought one and opened a publication office in Mladá Boleslav (Jungbunzlau). Before 1510, 60 printed works had appeared in Bohemia, and of these 50 or more were from the press of the Unity.

John Augusta, who was elected a bishop of the Unity in 1532, did not have a classical education in his youth, but when he decided to become a priest he took up the study of the Latin language and mastered it. He became Bohemia's most distinguished preacher, earning the title of "the Bohemian Luther."

The final period of the ancient Unitas Fratrum was marked by the leadership of two barons who helped maintain the high standard of education.

Baron Budova, of Bohemia, was a man of splendid talents and illustrious learning. He was greatly interested in the University of Prague, which had lost its position of preeminence but took on new life about this time. Baron Budova met death as a hero of the faith on the Day of Blood, June 21, 1621, in Prague.

To Baron John Zerotin, of Moravia, belongs much of the credit for the publication of the Kralice Bible, which "presented the Bohemian tongue [the Czech language today] in words more idiomatic, beautiful, and chaste than other books." For this great work Zerotin bore all the expense. Young men were sent to the universities of Wittenberg and Basel for preparation, and when they returned to Bohemia they translated the Old Testament from the Hebrew. The Unitas Fratrum printed this translation in five large volumes. A sixth volume contained the New Testament. The six volumes appeared at intervals from 1579 to 1593.

During the Thirty Years War, 1618-48, and the Counter-Reformation that followed, Protestant churches in Bohemia were closed, congregations were scattered, their members driven into exile, and the schools which had given to the Unity so widespread a reputation came to an end.

During the hundred years that followed, the educational activities of the Unitas Fratrum centered in one man, Bishop John Amos Comenius. Born March 28, 1592, in Moravia and educated in the schools of the Unity and at the University of Heidelberg, he became active in the Unitas Fratrum and was ordained into the priesthood at the Synod of 1616. The same Synod drew up the *Ratio Disciplinae,* a Book of Order, setting forth the constitution, ministry, ritual, and discipline of the Unitas Fratrum. This book played an important part in the reorganization of the Unitas Fratrum more than a century later.

When the persecutions that followed the Day of Blood sent thousands of members of the Unitas Fratrum into exile, Comenius lingered in Bohemia and Moravia, serving those who for one reason or another had remained behind. In 1628 he transferred his residence to Lissa in Poland, which for a while was a center of the Unitas Fratrum; there in 1632 Comenius was consecrated a bishop.

From then on, for the rest of his life, Comenius served not only the Unitas Fratrum but the entire world, earning the title of "father of modern education."

Educators of his day found his ideas new, even revolutionary:

> *Children must learn not only words, but also objects along with the words. Not the memory alone ought to be cultivated, but likewise the reasoning power, the will, the affections. Children should be taught to think clearly and to order their thoughts properly; at the same time an affectionate conversation with them should be kept up.*

Through his correspondence with scholars in various countries and through the books he wrote, his ideas spread and improved entire educational systems, especially in Poland, England, Sweden, and Holland. Tradition has it that he was invited to go to America as president of Harvard College, recently established, but he declined because he had promised to go to Sweden to reorganize its schools.

Of his books only four can be mentioned. *Orbis Pictus* (World in Pictures) made the amazing suggestion that pictures in a book increased its educational value. *Janua Linguarum Reserata* (Gate of Languages Unlocked) made his name known throughout Europe, in various parts of Asia, and even in the British colonies of America. *Informatorium* (School of Infancy) was written for the preschool child's instruction and is a handbook for Christian mothers. It initiated Comenius' plan "to build a fairer world through education."

Most important for the Moravian Church, Comenius translated the *Ratio Disciplinae* of 1616 into Latin, so making available this contemporary account of the customs, ritual, and discipline of the ancient Unitas Fratrum. Later, Buddaeus, of the University of Jena, translated it into German, and so it came into the hands of Count Zinzendorf when the destiny of the renewed Unitas Fratrum hung in the balance and turned the scales in favor of its reorganization.

Count Zinzendorf, on whose estates the Unitas Fratrum was reorganized, was a man of brilliant mind and wide learning. He was first educated by private tutors, then at the boarding school in Halle, at the University of Wittenberg, and by the customary year of travel which took him as far as Paris. His studies in philosophy, jurisprudence, theology, and oratory all contributed to his preparation for what was to be his life work. He had a genius for languages, spoke Latin fluently, and into his numerous writings, both prose and poetry, he was accustomed to inject Latin words and phrases, and words from the Greek, English, and French, whenever he thought such words gave a finer shade to the meaning he desired to express.

Naturally such a man would see to it that the children and youth under his care had every educational advantage that it was possible to give them. In Germany and in England schools were begun for girls as well as boys, and many of them continued through the years, rendering efficient service to members and friends.

Foremost among those who founded the Moravian Church in America stood August Gottlieb Spangenberg, a master of arts from the University of Jena, a professor at Halle, and a bishop of the Unitas Fratrum. He had much to do with arrangements during the early years in Pennsylvania, and he saw to it that schools were established there, again for girls as well as for boys.

Indeed, the first school established by Moravians in Pennsylvania was for girls. It was begun in Germantown by Benigna von Zinzendorf, in 1742, while she and her father were visiting in America. After she returned to Europe the school was moved to Bethlehem, where it still exists as the Moravian Academy, the successor of the earlier school. Another school for girls, which has continued until the present, is Linden Hall, begun in 1794 at Lititz, Pennsylvania.

A theological seminary was opened at Nazareth, Pennsylvania, in 1807, and after several interruptions it was moved to Bethlehem in 1858, and a college for men was also begun. In 1953 the Moravian College for Women was consolidated with Moravian College for Men into a coeducational institution under one administration.

Moravians brought education even into the frontier forests of North Carolina. In 1772 Salem was only a tiny village. But on its Board of Elders were three men trained in the universities of Europe, John Michael Graff and Paul Tiersch at Jena, and Frederic William Marshall at Leipzig. They cared so much for education that they provided a school for boys in 1771 and a school for girls in 1772, though the children were still of so tender an age that in most places their teaching would have been overlooked. The boys school lasted until 1910 and was succeeded by efficient city schools.

People visiting Salem in the early days, when the education of girls was not attempted elsewhere in the South, begged for years to let their daughters come to Salem to attend school. Finally, in 1802, their request was granted and plans were made for adding a boarding department to Salem's girls school. In the course of time the primary grades were dropped, and the school grew to become Salem Academy and College with a preparatory program in the academy and a full four-year liberal arts program in the college.

One more pioneer may be mentioned, Ludwig David von Schweinitz, who was born in Pennsylvania, educated in Europe, and served the Moravian Church in America from 1812 to his death in 1834. Though the ministry was his vocation, botany was his avocation. From childhood he was interested in fungi, and in 1817 the University of Kiel, Germany, gave him the degree of doctor of philosophy for his discoveries. He is said to have been the first man born in America to be awarded the doctor of philosophy degree. He is also recognized today as the "father of American mycology."

Moravian Archives

From the beginning, leaders of the Moravian Church have known the value of accurate historical records and have kept and preserved them.

The earliest archives of the Unitas Fratrum, however, were subjected to unusual accidents. The first collection of documents was destroyed at the end of the 15th century; the second perished in a fire in 1546. The great mass of their publications fell prey to the fury of the Counter-Reformation. Taking into consideration the disasters that befell the records and the persistent efforts that were made to blot them from existence, it is surprising that so much is known of the origin, episcopacy, and earliest history of the ancient Unitas Fratrum.

The synod of 1549 ordered that "all official letters and other historical documents are to be carefully collected and preserved." Most of this collection escaped the great conflagration which destroyed Lissa in Poland in 1656. At that time Lissa was the headquarters of the survivors of the ancient Unitas Fratrum and the residence of Bishop John Amos Comenius. Some of the papers were lost in Berlin, but a sizable portion of the Lissa papers was preserved and came to rest in the 19th century in the Unity Archives at Herrnhut.

The General Synod of 1764 provided for the continued care of the Archives of the Unity at Herrnhut. The Unity Synod of 1995 reaffirmed that the Archives at Herrnhut are the "special responsibility" of the entire Unity.

In the early days of the renewed Moravian Church ministers kept daily diaries and sent copies of them to the central boards of the Unity. At the European headquarters a board of secretaries reviewed these diaries and reports from the congregations and from mission fields, and made copies of them. In like manner copies were made of the memoirs, or biographical sketches of members, or accounts of important occurrences in the life of the Church, and of sermons preached by leading

Moravian ministers. These copies were called the *Gemein Nachrichten,* which served as a manuscript church newspaper sent to subscribers to be eagerly read in nearer and more distant parts of the Unity.

In addition local congregations kept minutes of their church boards, church registers, memoirs, and memorabilia. As these were deposited in the archives of each province, the collection increased in value. Few other churches have archive collections which in size, scope, and historical importance equal those of the Moravian Church.

Moravian Archives have been established during the past two and a half centuries in Herrnhut, Germany; Bad Boll, Germany; Prague, Czech Republic; London, England; Zeist, Holland; Genadendal, South Africa; Bethlehem, Pennsylvania; and Winston-Salem, North Carolina. To these centers congregations have sent their older records for safekeeping, and for proper filing, retaining only current records for present use.

Moravian Music Foundation

The Archives in Bethlehem, Pennsylvania, and Winston-Salem, North Carolina, are the repositories of still another collection of documents of historical significance. These are musical compositions, many in manuscript form dating back to colonial times. Much of this music was written by Moravian ministers; some of it was copied from music of European composers. It was the rediscovery of this collection that led to the establishment of the Moravian Music Foundation.

Founded in 1956 with its headquarters in Winston-Salem, North Carolina, the Moravian Music Foundation seeks to preserve the approximately 10,000 musical documents dating from the 18th and 19th centuries. In addition, the music collection has been cataloged and microfilmed for preservation. Among its other activities, the Foundation prepares modern scholarly editions of music from the collections; encourages research by making material available to qualified scholars; issues recordings; prepares music for use in Moravian Music Festivals, which are sponsored by the Northern and Southern Provinces every few years; works with Moravian congregations in music and worship resources; and distributes a quarterly newsletter as well as other specialized publications to keep historians, musicians, and supporters informed of activities. The Moravian musical heritage has gained wide renown through the Foundation, which since the mid-1950's has seen some two million copies of music sold. Moravian music is recognized as of great significance in the wider American musical landscape, and interest among European scholars in Moravian music is growing.

A LITURGICAL CHURCH

Liturgies

The Moravian Church is counted among the Protestant churches generally referred to as "liturgical churches." Liturgy means "a prepared form of prayer that includes participation on the part of the congregation." It was to provide for this participation and to give form and order to worship that liturgies came into use in the early Christian Church.

The Moravian Church has adopted for its use many of the liturgical forms of other churches. The Renewed Church, for example, took over many of the liturgies of the Lutheran Church of Germany. The Moravian Church has also developed a number of liturgies that are distinctively Moravian. One of these is the Liturgy for Easter Morning.

The *Moravian Book of Worship*, published in 1995, under the general heading of "The Liturgies," lists a total of 36 services. These are a General Liturgy for use with the Litany, the Church Litany, and a Shorter Church Litany; liturgies of Reconciliation, Adoration, Creation, Grace, Discipleship, and Celebration; 23 liturgies for the Church Year and Topical Liturgies; and four liturgies for the Rites and Sacraments of the Church. A Psalms and Canticles section includes *Benedictus*,

Magnificat, Gloria in Excelsis, Te Deum Laudamus, Christ Our Passover, St. Patrick's Hymn, This Is the Feast, Hosanna, Nunc Dimittis, and *Festal Doxology*. The *Festal Doxology*, to be used on the great festivals of the Church and on other special occasions, is really a hymn or anthem, and appeared first in Moravian hymnals in 1759.

The Litany

The word "litany" is of Greek origin and means "to ask." It finally came to mean a series of petitions made in public worship with responses by the people. This form was used first in the Greek Church and then in the Latin Church, especially in ecclesiastical processions, where priests at the head of the procession chanted a petition and the congregation following chanted the response.

The members of the Unitas Fratrum, when they organized in 1457, dropped many of the prevailing church forms as part of their protest against certain practices of the Roman Catholic Church, and their first hymnal, published in 1505, did not contain a litany. The first ancient Unity hymnal to have one was in 1571, and it was based on the litany that Martin Luther adapted from the Roman Catholic Church. (The Shorter Church Litany on pages 10-12 of the 1995 *Moravian Book of Worship* is based upon this 1571 litany of the ancient Unity.) The litany appeared in the first hymnal of the renewed Moravian Church in 1735, and it was natural that it too was modeled on Luther's litany, since Count Zinzendorf had grown up in the Lutheran Church. It was translated into English in 1754, and at that time a distinctly Moravian practice appeared. Hymns for congregational singing were introduced in both the German and English language litany.

Over the years, though a number of minor revisions have been made — specific petitions added, dropped, or modified —

the basic form of the litany remains the same in our most recent hymnal, the 1995 *Book of Worship*, as it was in the 1735 German hymnal. The *Kyrie Eleison* (Lord, have mercy upon us) begins the litany; it has come down from the earliest days of the Christian Church. The deprecations, prayers to be preserved *from* the evils named, and the obsecrations, prayers to be helped *by* what the Lord has done, are distinctly characteristic of a litany, differing from an order of worship or liturgy. The prayer, "Grant that all of us may pattern our lives…," compresses into one the petitions which formerly were offered for each Choir, or class, of the congregation. The prayer for the people of Israel and Islam and for "persons of every religion" asks the Lord to grant to all people, not just ourselves, "a fuller knowledge of your truth and love." The litany ends with the *Agnus Dei* (Christ, the Lamb of God) and a repetition of the *Kyrie* (O Christ, hear us).

Prefacing the litany in the 1995 *Book of Worship* is the General Liturgy 1, containing several creedal statements of Scripture and the early Church. The prayer of confession offered by the congregation, "We, like sheep, have gone astray," (Isa. 53:6) is followed by a distinctly Moravian response by the minister, who, still kneeling, says, "Thus says the Lord…" (Isa. 43:25; John 8:11). This indicates that it is the Lord who forgives sin, and the Lord only. Following the *Credo* (the Apostles' Creed) comes the *Gloria Patri* (Glory be to the Father), a very old chant. Then comes the *Pater Noster* (the Lord's Prayer), which originally was sung or chanted in the litany.

The hymns accompanying the litany and its prefacing liturgy are significant not only to the universal Church but to Moravians themselves. The first hymn in General Liturgy 1, "Worship, honor, glory, blessing," is by Englishman Edward Osler, and it is set to one of the most popular hymn tunes of the renewed Moravian Church. "O Lord, have mercy on us all" comes from the undivided Christian Church of the fourth century, attributed to Ambrose of Milan, the "father of Latin hymnody." In the litany itself "Most holy Lord and God" is a ninth century hymn based upon the *Trisagion,* the ancient Eastern Orthodox hymn to the Holy Trinity. It is a great confession of the deity of Christ and of the Atonement, cardinal points of Moravian — and Christian — faith. The hymn "Lord, for thy coming us prepare" expresses our faith in the second coming of Christ and how we await him. This stanza was written by Christian Gregor, organist at Herrnhut, member of the Unity Elders' Conference, and Moravian bishop. The Moravian Church owes much of its distinctive chorale form of music to Christian Gregor.

Moravian Hymns

One of the most striking features of the Moravian Church is our hymns. There are rarely more sublime occasions than a congregation's sonorous four-part singing of a beloved hymn. Visitors often comment on the beauty of that portion of a service.

Though new styles of music and contemporary hymns have been introduced in Moravian churches, many of the hymns date from Bishop Gregor's 1784 tunebook. Some are from the early years of the Reformation, and a few reach back as far as the ancient Christian Church of the fourth century.

Moravian hymns are more than just a moment for congregational singing. Often their words express the Moravian faith better than any creedal statement.

Baptism

Baptism is one of the two sacraments — the other is holy communion — of the Moravian Church, instituted by Christ Jesus, during which we experience the very real presence of the Savior. Infants as well as adults are baptized into the Church, the visible expression of the Lord's kingdom here on earth, using appropriate sections of the baptism liturgy as found in the 1995 *Book of Worship.*

For the baptism of children, they are presented by the parents, who with sponsors publicly declare their intention to lead the children "by prayer, instruction, and example toward that time when they can by grace confirm their faith in the Lord Jesus Christ and commit themselves to the life and work of the church." The congregation too promises to "affirm these children of God as members" and to accept its "obligation to love and nurture them in Christ."

For adult baptism those who have not been baptized in infancy make public profession of faith in Christ and their desire to "participate actively in Christ's church, serving God" all the days of their life. By adult baptism persons become full communicant members in the Church, and in some congregations sponsors are selected who assist the new members in becoming better acquainted with Christian life and customs of the Church.

As in all evangelical churches baptism is administered "in the name of the Father, and of the Son, and of the Holy Spirit" (Matt. 28:19). For more than 250 years the Moravian Church has introduced these words with the phrase "into the death of Jesus I baptize you." The Synod of 1751 explained that this was "Biblical and necessary, as otherwise there is no reference to the human life of our Savior, and the Apostle expressly said that those who were baptized were baptized into His death" (Rom. 6:3-4).

The Church Order, adopted by the Unity Synod of 1995, states, "Baptisms are, as a rule, to be performed in public meetings of the Church." Only in the case of emergencies are exceptions made to this rule.

Confirmation

Confirmation is a rite of the Church by which persons baptized in infancy confirm their baptismal covenant by making a public profession of faith in Jesus and then receive the blessing of the Lord. This rite admits them to full voting membership of a congregation.

The rite of confirmation was practiced in the ancient Unitas Fratrum. In the renewed Unitas Fratrum it was used for a candidate prior to the Lord's Supper on the Thirteenth of August 1727, but it did not come into general use in the Moravian Church until about 1751.

Candidates for confirmation are carefully instructed by the minister in the doctrines of the Christian faith. They examine their personal faith in Christ and their desire to become faithful members of the congregation.

In the Moravian Church a deacon, presbyter, or bishop may officiate at the service of confirmation. Certain questions (found on pages 170 and 171 in the *Book of Worship*) are addressed to the candidates and are answered by them. Then the candidates kneel, the minister lays hands on their head, recites a text selected as a watchword for each candidate, and pronounces the Old Testament benediction, which in the Moravian Church is always closed with the addition of the New Testament phrase "In the name of Jesus. Amen."

The Lord's Supper

Having dealt with baptism as a sacrament of the Moravian Church, we now turn to the other sacrament, the holy communion. The form in which the Lord's Supper is administered in the Moravian Church differs from that in any other church and goes back directly to the earliest years of the ancient Unitas Fratrum, when communicants stood to receive the sacraments as a protest against the Catholic "adoration of the host."

Generally in a Moravian congregation the communicants do not go forward to the communion table to partake, but the bread and cup are brought to them by the officiating minister. In the Moravian Church in North America wafers of unleavened bread are the custom. The minister places a wafer into the ungloved right hand of each communicant, who receives it standing. The congregation sings until all have been served, then the communicants partake, all standing, and then enter into silent prayer.

Formerly a large communion cup was passed from hand to hand along each pew. Today congregations generally use the individual service. The cup also is received standing. The congregation again sings until all are served, then they partake standing and have silent prayer. At the beginning and again at the close of the service of holy communion, the communicants give the "right hand of fellowship," the modern-day replacement for the kiss of peace. The right hand of fellowship following the opening prayer signifies "oneness in Christ." At the close it signifies "renewed dedication and unity of purpose in the service of Christ."

In the 1970's the Southern Province began agitating for a return to the ancient Christian practice of allowing baptized children to partake of communion before they were confirmed. The Unity Synods of 1981 and 1988 gave permission for each province to determine its own practice in this regard. Today churches of the Northern and Southern Provinces permit baptized children to partake of holy communion on request of parents and after receiving proper instruction.

The *Moravian Book of Worship* gives four series of hymns suitable for use in communion with a supplemental communion booklet containing four more. The hymns were selected in such a way that each series carries out a definite line of thought. Some are intended for special anniversaries, others for general occasions. All, of course, bear directly on the Lord's Supper and its meaning for Christians.

> *Jesus, we thus obey*
> *Your last and kindest word,*
> *And in your own appointed way*
> *We come to meet you, Lord.*

From the beginning, the Moravian Church has declined to enter into controversy concerning the manner of Christ's presence in the Lord's Supper, and the words of institution are the words Jesus used when he gave the bread and cup to His disciples, omitting any human interpretation (Matt. 26:26-27, Mark 14:22-24, Luke 22:19-20, 1 Cor. 11:23-26).

Communicant members of other denominations are welcome to partake of the Lord's Supper with any Moravian congregation.

The Surplice

Both the ancient Unity and the renewed Moravian Church were slow to introduce the surplice. In 1609, when the Unitas Fratrum had formed a federation with Lutheran and Reformed Churches in Bohemia, some ministers of the Unity followed the Lutherans and wore a surplice when preaching and when administering the sacraments. In the renewed Moravian Church the surplice was not introduced until 1748. Its color is white, as Zinzendorf put it, in anticipation of becoming pure souls through the merits of the Savior (Rev. 1:13; 7:9; 19:8). The Sisters, he said, had led the way in the white dresses they wore on special church occasions.

By wearing a surplice ministers indicate that they have eliminated themselves, and that in the sacrament or rite which is being performed the blessings must come directly from God. Therefore the surplice is used properly when baptizing an infant or an adult, when giving the confirmation blessings, when administering the holy communion, for ordinations, and for consecrations. It may also be used at the solemnization of matrimony, because the minister may solemnize it only as an or-dained servant of Christ and may consecrate the union only in the name of the Lord.

chapter III

THE CHURCH YEAR

The Church Year

Through the years many customs and practices have so fixed themselves in the life and services of the Moravians that they have come to be considered distinctive of the Moravian Church. Some of these are memorial days belonging to the Moravian Church alone, and they will be discussed in our next chapter. Others belong to the church universal and are observed by several other churches besides the Moravian, but the Moravian Church has given to them certain features which differ from those in other churches.

The church year was developed gradually during the first 600 years of Christianity. Church leaders felt the need of a definite schedule for the study of the life of Christ and essential features of Christian faith, and so various plans were tried and various dates selected. The first step was the selection of Sunday, the day on which the Lord Jesus Christ rose from the tomb, as the beginning of the Christian week. In the course of time the Sunday falling on or closest to St. Andrew's Day, November 30, was selected as the beginning of the church year, allowing four Sundays of preparation for the great Christmas festival.

Along with the development of the church year, special passages of Scripture were assigned to each Sunday to contribute toward spiritual growth. The Old Testament passages followed Jewish custom, where set lessons from the Law and the Prophets were read, as they were read by the Lord when he spoke in the synagogue at Nazareth. New series of lessons from the Epistles and Gospels were added to follow the schedule of the new Christian church year.

These lessons were called the *pericopes*, a Greek word meaning "to cut around," in other words selected extracts. For over 1,400 years, with a few slight alterations, these same lessons have been used by the Roman Catholic Church, the Church of England, the Episcopal, Lutheran, Reformed, and Moravian Churches. In the American Episcopal Church the pericopes are read in the communion service. In Moravian churches they are usually read during the regular service of worship, though their use is not required and ministers are free to vary from this practice.

During the 1970's at the initiative of the Roman Catholic Church, a three-year lectionary was developed. Rather than reading only one year's worth of Scriptures, three years' worth was selected, allowing congregations to hear a broader scope of the Bible. With only a few variations, Episcopal, Lutheran, Reformed, and Moravian Churches have also adopted the expanded lectionary so that on any given Sunday the same Scriptures are heard in all these denominations — a strong act of unity among the many different branches of Christ's Body, His Church here on earth.

Advent

The church year does not coincide with the secular calendar year, but begins four Sundays before Christmas Day, with the First Sunday in Advent.

Advent is a Latin word, meaning "coming," and was chosen

to designate the four weeks of preparation for the celebration of the birth of Christ. Advent Sundays present in various combinations the themes of Christ's coming and our human response: in the past as recorded in the Scriptures, in the present to our hearts, and in glory in the future at the end of time.

Of the two Moravian liturgies for the season one is titled Advent and Palm Sunday (since both stress Christ's coming), with portions appropriate for either occasion. In all, it is a grand program of praise to the coming Savior. The opening hymn,

> *Hail to the Lord's anointed,*
> *Great David's greater Son!*
> *Hail, in the time appointed*
> *His reign on earth begun!*

was written by the English Moravian, James Montgomery, and strikes the keynote for the entire service. The Advent and Palm Sunday liturgy provides a place for the singing of "Hosanna," the anthem composed by Christian Gregor in 1783 (page 239 in the *Book of Worship*). Another "Hosanna," also sung antiphonally, was composed by Edward Leinbach, a Moravian musician of Winston-Salem, North Carolina. It has been published and a number of congregations use it during the Advent season and on Palm Sunday. The Advent 2 liturgy, apart from its hymns, is largely composed of petitions of joy, contrition, and praise.

> *Our hope and expectation,*
> *O Jesus, now appear!*
> *Arise, the sun so longed for*
> *O'er this benighted sphere!*

In some Moravian churches the hymn, "Morning Star," is sung antiphonally on the Third or Fourth Sunday in Advent. In most churches it is also used on Christmas Eve. The hymn was written by Johann Scheffler (1624-77), a physician of Silesia, who took the name Angelus on joining the Roman Catholic

Church where he became a priest. A new tune for the hymn was composed in 1836 by Francis F. Hagen, a Moravian born and raised in Salem who became a minister, and it was published as sheet music in 1857 with words translated by Martin Hauser, a Moravian minister living in Illinois. Another translation was done in 1885 by the English Moravian minister Bennett Harvey, Jr., and this is the one that appeared in the American hymnals of 1908, 1923, and 1969. The 1995 *Book of Worship* has both versions, the familiar Bennett Harvey translation as hymn 281 and the anthem-like Martin Hauser translation as hymn 323. Both are set to the tune composed by Br. Hagen.

The Star

In many Moravian churches and homes a large many-pointed star is carefully preserved from year to year. With the approach of the Christmas season this star is brought out and hung in the sanctuary or in the hall or on the porch, where it remains until the Christmas decorations are taken down or until Epiphany. Sometimes it is an Advent Star, appearing on the First Sunday in Advent, heralding the approaching Christmas festival; sometimes it is a Christmas Star, reserved until the evergreens are placed for Christmas. Always it is a lighted star, shining to proclaim its message.

Who invented the "Moravian Star" is not known. Apparently it originated in the evening handicraft sessions at the paedagogium, or school, in Niesky, Germany, about 1850. In the 1880's Pieter Verbeek attended the paedagogium as a student; later he began to make the stars for sale, with the help of two or three young girls who worked at home. His son, Harry Verbeek, learned the art from his father, and later founded the Herrnhut star factory. The elder Verbeek made the earlier stars with points which could be fastened to a rigid metal core; later he and his son learned to make points which could be fastened together with paper fasteners. For some years the two Verbeeks had charge of the book store in Herrnhut, and there they received orders for the stars made in the star factory, which they shipped to many places, the directions for assembling them being printed in four languages. When war closed the Herrnhut star factory, Moravians in other areas also took up the business of supplying this much beloved Christmas emblem.

The Moravian Star has a three-fold message. It testifies to the greatness of the Creator who made the stars on the fourth day (Gen. 1:16), numberless (Gen. 15:5), differing in glory (1 Cor. 15:41), and praising the might that laid the foundations of the world (Job 38:7). It is a reminder of the star that once led the Wise Men from their distant homes "until it stopped over the place where the Child was," and they fell down before Him and worshipped Him (Matt. 2:2, 7, 9, 10). It points to the Divine Star, foretold by the prophet who said, "A Star shall come out of Jacob" (Num. 24:17), and fulfilled in Him who said of Himself, "I am the root and descendant of David, the bright morning star" (Rev. 22:16).

> *Light of the world, into our hearts*
> *Let Thy full glory shine,*
> *That we may follow now Thy star*
> *Until we reach Thy shrine.*
>
> *1969 hymnal, 71*

The Putz, Candle Tea, and the Advent Wreath

The German word Putz simply means a decoration, but North American Moravians use it in a special way to mean a distinctive kind of Christmas decoration. Probably the idea came from the Church of the Middle Ages, when priests placed figures of the Holy Family in the churches so that their unlettered people might get a clearer idea of the Christmas story. Whatever the origin, the Moravian settlers brought the idea with them to America at an early date. In Bethlehem, Pennsylvania, the Putz is a long-cherished custom, and as early as 1760 a "Christmas decoration" was made in Bethabara, North Carolina.

In its simplest form the Putz is a reminder of the manger scene in the cave stable of Bethlehem. In some Moravian families the nativity figures are heirlooms; in others they are beautifully carved figures imported from abroad; in still others they are quite new and have been bought at a department store. The nativity figures form the center of the Putz. Other items are often added, such as the sheep on a neighboring hillside, or the approaching Magi. Beyond this, individual fancy plays. The Putz may be on the floor at the foot of a decorated Christmas tree; or it may be on a small table with only a bit of evergreen as a background. Always its purpose is to tell the story of the first Christmas in Bethlehem of Judea.

A custom associated with the Putz developed in Salem in the 1930's and came to be called the Candle Tea. An Advent tradition, the Candle Tea is sponsored by the Women's Fellowships of a number of churches and can include candle making demonstrations, hymn singing, and refreshments, as well as the story of the birth of Jesus told in a Putz.

Another custom borrowed from other denominations has gained popularity in Moravian homes and churches. This is the Advent wreath. Four candles are arranged in a wreath of greenery, and often a fifth one is in the center. On each Sunday of Advent, the appropriate number of outer candles is lit, one on the First Sunday of Advent, two on the Second Sunday, and so forth. The center candle is lit with all the four outer ones on Christmas Day. As to the meaning of the candles, opinions vary since this custom is fairly new. They can stand for hope, peace, joy, and love; or they can mean our preparation, the coming of the Lord, sharing of Christ's love, and the glad tidings of His birth; or they can be tied to the Scriptures of the lectionary readings assigned for each Advent Sunday. The center candle, lit on Christmas Day, is the Christ child.

Christmas Eve

No special liturgy is provided for Christmas Eve, but most Moravian congregations celebrate the day with a candle service using the lighted wax tapers or Moravian Christmas candles. Because of the large number of people attending, it is often necessary for the congregations to hold two or more of these services. In some churches one of the services is planned especially for children. Many congregations combine a lovefeast with the candle service.

Christmas Candles

The Moravians' use of lighted wax tapers at the Christmas Eve lovefeast has been traced to the 1747 service for the children of Marienborn held by Br. Johannes von Watteville. The *Gemein Diarium* (Unity Diary) tells the story:

> *A hymn was sung. Br. Johannes asked questions concerning the birth of Jesus, and the children answered. [The questions and answers were lines from hymns familiar to the children, and are given in the Diary account.] Then Br. Johannes spoke of the inexpressible blessedness which came through the birth of Jesus; among other things that by His wounds and pierced side he had lighted a blood-red flame of love in every heart, which would burn forever to His joy and our salvation. For an impressive reminder of this, each child was to receive a burning taper, tied with a small red ribbon.... Then the children held their tapers aloft and Br. Johannes sang Does your heart burn? and also*

O little Jesus, Thee I love!
Kindle a pure and holy flame
Within the heart of every child,
Like that which from Thine own heart came.

The idea found quick acceptance in the Moravian Church. Herrnhut held a similar service the following year. In North America the first use of candles on Christmas Eve was in 1756 in Bethlehem, Pennsylvania. In North Carolina the Christmas candles were used for the first time in the children's lovefeasts of Bethabara and Bethania in 1762. In all these services the emphasis was on the love of Jesus, which led Him to come as the Babe of Bethlehem, prepared to atone for humanity, and the response which should be a flame of love in the heart of every child. Today it stresses rather the light which came into the world with the birth of Christ and the response which every Christian should make by witnessing for Him.

Since around the beginning of the 20th century a paper frill, most often red and non-inflammable if possible, is wrapped around each candle. Not only does the frill protect hands from any wax burn, but the red reminds us of the blood of Christ shed for us all.

A tradition that is popular in the British Province is the Christingle. At Christmas services oranges topped by lighted candles are distributed to the children. The orange symbolizes the round world, and the candle is the Christ child, the light of the world come on this day. A hymn in the 1995 *Book of Worship* tells the significance of the Christingle: "O Round as the World Is the Orange."

Christmas Day

For Christmas a beautiful liturgy is provided in the *Book of Worship*. It consists largely of quotations from the Bible, and the centerpiece is the *Magnificat*, Mary's song of praise that God has "looked with favor on the lowliness of his servant" (Luke 1:47-55). The liturgy closes with two verses of the hymn "Christ the Lord, the Lord most Glorious," written by Moravian minister John Miller and set to a tune composed by Salem's Edward Leinbach. Many churches close their Christmas Eve services with this hymn. The verses were used in Salem as early as 1807, less than two decades after they were first published in the 1789 *British Moravian hymnal.*

Though some congregations have a service on Christmas Day, as a rule this liturgy is used on the Sunday nearest Christmas Day. All three yearly cycles of the lectionary unite into one set of Scripture lessons for Christmas Day — Isa. 52:7-10; Psalm 98; Heb. 1:1-4, (5-12); John 1:1-14 — all emphasizing the incarnation. The deep spiritual value of the Christmas festival is that it celebrates the greatest miracle of all ages, when God became incarnate.

Epiphany

Tradition says that it was on January 6 that the Wise Men came to Bethlehem, following the star which led them to Him "who has been born King of the Jews."

The word Epiphany means manifestation, revelation, a showing forth. The message of Epiphany, as shown in the Gospel lesson for the day (Matt. 2:1-12), is the manifestation of Christ to the Wise Men from the east.

The Moravian liturgy for Epiphany is therefore distinctly and appropriately a missionary liturgy and is titled Epiphany and World Mission. A congregation may well appoint the day as a mission festival, or a mission rally later in the year may use the Epiphany liturgy. Indeed it is appropriate for opening any missionary gathering, large or small.

Epiphany is followed in the church year by up to nine

Sundays after Epiphany, though the fifth through ninth Sundays are frequently omitted because of the movable date of Easter. The whole Epiphany season presents the progressive manifestation of the Lord from His baptism by John and the Spirit descending upon him like a dove to the Last Sunday after Epiphany, which in the current church calendar is Transfiguration Sunday (Matt. 17:1-9; Mark 9:2-9; Luke 9:28-36, (37-43)).

The last three Sundays after Epiphany in the new three-year lectionary were known in earlier times by the Latin names indicating the number of days before Easter, not counting the Sundays. *Septuagesima* falls within the 70-day period; *Sexagesima* is 60 days; *Quinquagesima*, 50 days (now called Transfiguration Sunday).

Lent

Ash Wednesday, 40 days before Easter, not counting Sundays, is the beginning of Lent. The name comes from a custom in the early Roman Catholic Church of making the sign of the cross on the foreheads of penitents using the ashes of palms brought to church on Palm Sunday of the preceding year.

The traditional Latin names of the Sundays in Lent are the opening words of the Psalms which were chanted in the ancient church on those special days: The First Sunday in Lent is *Invocavit*, Psalm 91:15: He shall *call upon me....* The Second Sunday is *Reminiscere*, Psalm 25:6: *Remember*, O Lord.... The Third Sunday is *Oculi*, Psalm 25:15: *Mine eyes....* The Fourth Sunday is *Laetare*, Isaiah 66:10: *Rejoice* ye with Jerusalem.... The Fifth Sunday is *Judica*, Psalm 43:1: *Judge* me, O God....

The sixth Sunday of Lent is Palm Sunday, which begins Holy Week, or Passion Week as it was also earlier called. Many Moravian churches have made it a custom to hold adult baptism and confirmation on Palm Sunday, though the recent trend is to return those rites of admission to the church to the more traditional Pentecost, the "birthday" of the Christian church. It should be noted that in the Moravian Church baptisms, confirmations, and receptions are not limited to Palm Sunday or Pentecost and may occur at any time during the church year.

The *Moravian Book of Worship* has two liturgies for Lent. One, a more traditional one, is little changed from, say, the 1876 hymnal. The other Lenten liturgy is more contemporary in concept and pattern. For Palm Sunday we return to the Advent and Palm Sunday liturgy in the *Book of Worship*. The Palm Sunday portions speak of Jesus' triumphal entry into Jerusalem as we again sing hosannas at His coming.

Holy Week

There are three distinctive features of Holy Week in the Moravian Church: the reading meetings, the Holy Thursday communion, and the Great Sabbath lovefeast, now generally held on Good Friday.

The reading meetings begin on the evening of Palm Sunday and continue through the Friday before Easter Sunday. In these meetings there is no address. The singing of a hymn and a prayer are followed by reading from the Holy Week Manual, a harmony of the Gospels covering the last week of the earthly life of the Lord. As early as 1770 it was customary to intersperse the reading at frequent intervals with congregational singing of suitable hymn stanzas. These stanzas are now printed in the manual. The accounts are read as close to the days of the week on which the events occurred, although since there is no account for Wednesday and the account of Tuesday is very long, adaptations have been made.

The evening of Holy Thursday is dedicated to the Lord's Supper, which was instituted by the Lord on the Thursday evening of the first Holy Week. In earlier times the day was called Maundy Thursday. The word Maundy comes from the Latin words *mandatum est*, "It is commanded," in remembrance of the "new commandment" given by Jesus on that evening (John 13:34). Moravians make every effort to attend this most holy communion, and members of other churches are invited to come to the table "of their Lord and ours."

On Good Friday the Savior is followed in thought to Calvary and to the tomb in Joseph's garden. A number of Moravian churches hold their crucifixion service in the afternoon, ending the reading at 3 o'clock, the time of the Savior's death on the cross. A postlude is not played, but rather the worshippers file out in utter silence. For indeed this service does not conclude here, but on Easter morn. No other service is as powerful and emotional as the crucifixion service.

In times past, Moravians held a lovefeast on Great Sabbath, the day before Easter, in memory of the Lord's rest in the grave. It was an appropriate transition from thoughts on the suffering of the Lord to the glory of His Resurrection. Recently churches have been holding their lovefeasts on Good Friday evening and incorporating in it the reading of the burial and sealing of the tomb. Like the earlier Great Sabbath lovefeasts, these Good Friday lovefeasts look forward to the glorious proclamation of the Resurrection that is to come Easter morning.

Holy Week Manual

A significant contribution of the Moravian Church to Christian thought and worship has been the harmony of the Gospels, and especially the Holy Week Manual. The first Moravian harmony of the Gospels was printed in Germany in 1757 and bore the title (in German) *The Story of the Days of the Son of Man, Compiled from the Four Gospels*. A note in the appendix states that "this may be the first attempt to prepare a harmony of the Gospels." A second edition of this harmony appeared in 1759, and a note on page 188 shows that the book was compiled by Count Zinzendorf.

It is said that Zinzendorf was well acquainted with the form of critical Bible study in which parallel passages were placed side by side on a page, but that he wanted a compilation which was suitable for devotional use, an idea that other Pietists also shared.

Zinzendorf was a fine linguist, so he did not rely on other translations of the Gospels but made his own when he thought he could improve on the Luther translation. This was not entirely satisfactory to those accustomed to the wording used by Luther, so in 1764, four years after the death of Zinzendorf, a new compilation of the Gospels was undertaken by Samuel Lieberkuehn, a Moravian minister highly esteemed for his knowledge of the Bible. Lieberkuehn used the Luther translation of the Bible and made some changes in chronology in accordance with the conclusions of certain contemporary Biblical scholars. For the Holy Week portion he divided the story, assigning each portion to its own day for the reading. Lieberkuehn's harmony was published in 1769. It was published in England in 1771, using the King James Version of the Bible. Lieberkuehn's harmony was also translated into the Delaware language by David Zeisberger, the great Moravian missionary to the Indians.

As for a separate *Holy Week Manual*, apparently one was also printed in England in 1771 and in Germany in 1775. Surprisingly, the Moravians in North America were the first to publish the separate *Holy Week Manual*. That was done in Philadelphia in 1769, the same year the first edition of Lieberkuehn's entire harmony appeared in Germany.

Lieberkuehn's compilation went through many editions, both in its entirety and as the separate *Holy Week Manual*. In North America a number of editions of the manual have been published. Currently the Northern and Southern Provinces have printed the 1995 edition, which uses the New Revised Standard

Version of the Bible and hymns for the most part from the 1995 *Moravian Book of Worship*. Some printings include the tunes to go with the hymns for easier singing.

Easter

Following the selection of Sunday as the day to celebrate Christ's Resurrection each week, the ancient Church next settled upon a day to celebrate the Resurrection during the entire year. To make it roughly coincide with the Jewish Passover, it was made a movable feast, and consequently the other days that were connected to it — Ash Wednesday, Lent, Holy Week, Ascension, and Pentecost — are also movable. In the Western Church the day is the first Sunday after the full moon on or after the vernal equinox (March 21). Thus the day can be as early as March 22 or as late at April 25. In England the day was given the name Easter, after a pagan goddess whose festival day was in the spring.

In many Moravian churches Easter is observed in a special way with a service held at sunrise, concluding in the graveyard. The idea originated in Herrnhut in 1732 with a group of young Brethren who had met for prayer on the preceding evening. They decided that "as it began to dawn toward the first day of the week" they, like the disciples, would go to the place of burial. Unlike the disciples, they knew that "the Lord is risen," and to Him they sang their hymns of praise.

The impromptu service of these young men proved so impressive that it became a custom, and it was brought to America by the early Moravian settlers who introduced it in their communities in colonial days. It is one of the most impressive and one of the most devotional services of the church year.

The service of Salem Congregation in Winston-Salem, North Carolina, may be given as illustrative of its observance, since it has come to be the most largely attended.

About two o'clock in the morning all the musicians who play in the Easter band assemble in groups and go throughout the city, playing Easter chorales, partly to waken people who will attend the sunrise service, and partly to remind all listeners of the Resurrection of which the music speaks.

The service itself begins in front of Home Church at Salem Square. There are no ceremonial trappings at this service, no cross. (The cross belonged to Good Friday; this is the day of Resurrection!) The entire service consists of the Easter Morning liturgy, which in the 1969 hymnal is labeled "A Confession of Faith." And indeed it is. From the speaker's stand comes the voice of the minister in charge: "The Lord is risen!" From the reverent multitude comes the response: "The Lord is risen indeed!" (Luke 24:35). Even so the disciples greeted each other in the first years after the first Easter dawn.

The service continues with a great statement of faith in the Triune God, patterned after the Nicene Creed with many passages from Scripture and two passages from Martin Luther's Small Catechism ("This is my Lord..."; "We believe that by our own reason and strength..."). Then in reverential procession the congregation moves from the church to God's Acre, about a block away. As they go, the musicians play Easter chorales antiphonally, answering each other until the last band has entered the central gate behind the congregation.

When all have gathered on the walks which surround the squares where lie those who have "fallen asleep in the Lord," the remainder of the liturgy is read, with the band leading the singing of the hymns.

> *The Spirit and the Bride*
> *"O come" are now entreating.*
> *1969 hymnal, p. 56 (Rev. 22:17)*

Aside from the Easter Morning liturgy, the *Moravian Book of Worship* also has a lovely Easter liturgy. It is generally used at the regular Easter Sunday worship, and it begins as an echo of the Easter Morning liturgy: The Lord is risen! The Lord is risen indeed! The opening hymn proclaims,

> *The day of resurrection!*
> *Earth, tell it out abroad,*

The liturgy closes with the triumphant hymn, "Sing hallelujah, praise the Lord!"

God's Acre

This name, in the Moravian acceptance of the term, does not mean an acre dedicated to God. It means "God's field," in which the bodies of Christians are laid awaiting the Resurrection.

In the old diaries the Moravians never said that a member had died; some more expressive phrase was always used. In the old church registers the column for the date of death was headed "Fell Asleep." The general heading for the death records was "Went Home and Was Laid in the Grave."

The Easter Morning liturgy, which is one of the oldest of the Moravian liturgies, carries out the same idea of a planted field, where "this perishable body must put on imperishability, and this mortal body must put on immortality."

Thus Moravian congregations established their own burial grounds and called their graveyards "God's Acre." They felt that only in a place of burial which was used by Christians was it fitting to hold the early Easter service and affirm belief in the resurrection of all through faith in the risen Christ.

A typical Moravian God's Acre has certain characteristics. It is laid off in rather large squares, and these squares are assigned to definite groups in the church family. Married women and widows are buried chronologically in one square; married men and widowers in another. Single men are on one side of a square, with little boys on the other side of the same square; single women and little girls share another square. The idea is that those who were most closely associated in life, whose interests and responsibilities gave them most in common, will want to be together in repose. In recent years in congregations where cremation has become an accepted practice, the section for these remains is laid out in the same manner of groups in the church family.

There are no monuments. On each grave is a slab of marble, bearing the name of the person interred there, the dates of birth and death, and often a Bible verse or a few suitable words. These gravestones are of uniform size for adults, somewhat smaller on the smaller graves of children and in the cremation section.

Traditionally all graves face the east. Formerly, whenever possible, the graveyard was placed on the slope of a hill facing the east. These, however, are customs, not rules.

Members of a Moravian congregation which has a typical Moravian God's Acre are not obligated to burial there. If an ordinary family plot is preferred and a cemetery of the usual type is available, there is no objection to the purchase and use of a family plot.

Usually, however, burial in God's Acre is considered a privilege. As a rule, the congregation bears the expense of the proper care of the area, including the individual graves, after the stones have been placed by the families.

Members of congregations which do not have such a God's Acre use the cemeteries or memorial parks of their communities.

Easter to Pentecost

The Sundays following Easter, like the Sundays of Lent, carry names taken from the Scripture read on those days in the ancient church. Easter Day itself is the first Sunday of Easter. The Second Sunday of Easter is *Quasimodogeniti*, 1 Pet. 2:2: *As newborn babes* desire the sincere milk of the word…. The Third Sunday of

Easter is *Misericordias*, Psalm 33:5: ...the earth is full of the *goodness [mercy]* of the Lord. The Fourth Sunday of Easter is *Jubilate*, Psalm 66:1: *Make a joyful noise* unto God.... The Fifth Sunday of Easter is *Cantate*, Psalm 98:1: *O sing* unto the Lord.... The Sixth Sunday of Easter is *Rogate*, Isaiah 48:20: ...the Lord had redeemed his servant Jacob. The Seventh Sunday of Easter is *Exaudi*, Psalm 27:7: *Hear*, O Lord, when I cry with my voice....

In the Moravian Church in North America the Fifth Sunday of Easter is celebrated as Moravian Music Sunday, frequently devoting the service to hymns and anthems composed or written by Moravians.

Ascension Day, 40 days after Easter, is the concluding portion of the *Holy Week Manual*, and brings to an end the account of His earthly ministry. Falling as it does on a Thursday in midweek, Ascension Day does not have a Sunday devoted to it. However, the *Moravian Book of Worship* has five hymns devoted to the day.

> Hail the day that sees him rise,
> To his throne above the skies.

Pentecost is when the Church celebrates its "birthday," the outpouring of the Holy Spirit upon the disciples, as recorded in Acts 2. The word Pentecost is from the Greek meaning 50, as Pentecost comes 50 days after Easter. The day is also known as Whitsunday, "white Sunday," because in the early Church candidates for baptism on that day wore white garments. The *Moravian Book of Worship* liturgy for the occasion is titled "Pentecost and Spiritual Renewal" and is devoted to the power and leading of the Holy Spirit of the Trinity.

Pentecost to Advent

The first Sunday after Pentecost is Trinity Sunday, and it is devoted to the consideration of the Triune God. From the First

Sunday in Advent until this Sunday the Church reflects upon the revelation of God as made known in the earthly life of Christ Jesus. The revelation of the facts of salvation culminates in the outpouring of the Holy Spirit as celebrated on Pentecost. Then the Church adds one more festival, Trinity Sunday, to reveal the constitution of the Godhead, which made the divine plan of salvation possible. God the Father evolved the plan; God the Son carried it out; God the Holy Spirit applies it to those who are being saved. The Trinity liturgy in the *Moravian Book of Worship* reflects upon the great truth of the Trinity through Scripture, prayer, and hymns.

Following Trinity Sunday the church year numbers the Sundays after Pentecost through the months until the last Sunday before Advent, which is known as Reign of Christ, or Christ the King Sunday. The liturgy for this Sunday is titled not only Reign of Christ but also Second Coming, and is devoted to the Lord, who will descend from heaven with a shout to fulfill the kingdom of God and reign as King of Kings and Lord of Lords. Thus the Advent season, which opens the church year, and Reign of Christ Sunday, which closes the year, both point to Christ's coming.

The Colors of the Church

Closely associated with the church year are the different colored pulpit Bible markers for each season, as adopted in the mid-20th century from the Episcopal Church. The seasons and their colors are purple or blue in Advent, white in the Christmas season, white on Epiphany Sunday and the Sunday before Ash Wednesday, green on the Sundays after Epiphany, purple on Ash Wednesday, purple or black in Lent, purple on Palm Sunday, purple or white on Maundy Thursday, purple or no Bible markers at all on Good Friday, white on Easter and the Sundays of Easter, red on Pentecost, white on Trinity Sunday, green on the Sundays after Pentecost, and white on Reign of Christ Sunday.

Colors for special days of the church year are red for the martyrdom of John Hus on July 6 and for the August Thirteenth Festival, white or red for All Saints' Day, white for the November Thirteenth Festival, and green for Thanksgiving Day.

The colors are not altered for baptisms, weddings, or funerals, since they are events in individuals' lives and do not affect the church year.

So far as is known the Moravian Church has never formally adopted colors, but red and white are generally accepted. This may have arisen with Count Zinzendorf, who wrote the hymn:

> *The Savior's blood and righteousness*
> *My beauty is, my glorious dress.*
> *Book of Worship, 201*

The colors, red (blood) and white (righteousness or purity), seem to be based on this hymn.

chapter IV

A CHURCH THAT REMEMBERS

March First

Since the exact date of the beginning of the Unitas Fratrum in 1457 has been lost, March 1 has been selected as the "birthday" of the Unity. No special observances are designated, but the date brings to remembrance the deeds of the spiritual forebears of the Moravian Church.

May Twelfth

May 12 is not commonly observed as a Moravian anniversary day, and yet three events of great significance are associated with the day. Count Zinzendorf once summed them up as follows:

> *The twelfth of June, 1722, was an undetermined matter, without signature or stamp. Those who came on May 12, 1724, bore the stamp which for 26 years the world has been trying to erase, but it did not succeed, for last year [1749] the Saviour confirmed it, sealed it, renewed it, and made it more effective than ever before.*

This rather quaint picture of the renewed Moravian Church as a legal document, first without signature or seal, then signed, then renewed and sealed, leads directly into the history of those days.

June 12, 1722, was the day on which the first emigrants from Moravia reached the estate of Count Zinzendorf in Upper Lusatia, now Saxony. The company consisted of only 11, counting men, women, and children, and of these only three were "housefathers." Their aims were vague; they had fled from a Roman Catholic country into a land where Protestants might live undisturbed, but their thoughts went little further than the gaining of religious freedom.

On May 12, 1724, five young men from Suchdol (Zauchtenthal), Moravia, arrived at Herrnhut, the little village which the immigrants of two years before were building. Three of them bore the same name, David Nitschmann, and in addition there were Melchior Zeisberger and Johann Toeltschig. All were descendants of the ancient Unitas Fratrum; all desired to live a religious life; all had been threatened with severe punishment if they continued to meet for divine worship and had been definitely forbidden to attempt to leave the country of their birth.

Faced with those alternatives they decided to risk emigration and slipped across the border of Moravia with nothing except their high purpose and dauntless courage.

They reached Herrnhut on May 12 and were disappointed to find it such a small place, but on the same day they attended the cornerstone laying for a large house which was being built for a boys school. They were so impressed with the spirit of the occasion that they decided to remain.

So great was the influence of these young men upon the history of the Moravian Church that they have come down in the records as "the five churchmen." One David Nitschmann went back to his native land to preach and suffered the death of a martyr. David Nitschmann, the carpenter, was one of the first two missionaries to the West Indies, became the first bishop of the renewed Unitas Fratrum, led to Pennsylvania the party which founded Bethlehem, and was one of the most influential leaders of the Church in Europe. David Nitschmann, the weaver, became the syndic, representing the Moravian Church in negotiations with the governments of various European states. Johann Toeltschig was one of the Moravian colonists in Georgia and served later in England and Ireland. Melchior Zeisberger also became a Moravian minister; he served many years in Denmark, but passed away in Herrnhut, the last of the five churchmen to leave their earthly labors for the kingdom of God.

The second major event on a May 12 was in 1727. On that day the entire community of Herrnhut adopted the *Brotherly Agreement*. Actually two events took place that day in Herrnhut. In one the residents gave their pledge of fidelity to Count Zinzendorf, who had recently bought the estate of Upper Berthelsdorf from his uncle, the Privy Counselor von Gersdorf.

Linked with the residents' pledge of loyalty was the other event on that day, their decision to accept the statutes, or *Brotherly Agreement*, which had been drawn up for their guidance. The Count called all of his tenants together, men and women, and spoke to them for three hours, explaining the statutes in great detail. He spoke with great earnestness of the evil of division and explained that each man and woman who wished to accept these statutes should give him his or her hand; those who did not wish to do so were to leave the village at once.

To the surprise of all present everybody accepted the statutes, called the *Brotherly Agreement* (now the *Moravian Covenant for Christian Living*). They promised to live for the Savior, expressed regret for the sectarian disputes in which they had been indulging, and agreed unanimously that from that day all sectarian differences should be ignored.

At that time the congregation of Herrnhut consisted of about 300 members, living in 34 houses. Probably two-thirds of the residents were immigrants from Moravia.

Writing 21 years later, Count Zinzendorf said that May 12, 1727, decided the question whether Herrnhut should adopt the plan of being a church of God, or should be merely a small village according to the will of man. The Holy Spirit led them to choose the first.

The third great event to occur on a May 12 was in 1749. It was then that Great Britain's Parliament passed the act which recognized the Moravian Church as an "ancient Protestant Episcopal Church" and gave it full church privileges in all British colonies. This act was of inestimable value for the work in America. According to Zinzendorf, the Moravians asked for an investigation by Parliament because acts had been passed in the colonies of New York and Virginia against any "Vagrant Preacher, Moravian or Disguised Papist" — this for the first Church to be organized in protest against certain practices of the papacy.

The 1749 act of Parliament nullified the New York act and made it impossible to use "anti-papist" acts against Moravians there or in Virginia. Probably its greatest value in the American colonies was in the Moravian settlement in North Carolina, which followed four years after the passing of the act. Under it the Moravians in Wachovia claimed and obtained their own parish, their own vestry, and full recognition of their ministerial orders, privileges accorded to no other church so long as North Carolina was a British colony and the Church of England was the established church. The American Revolution wiped out the distinctions between the Moravian Church and other churches.

July Sixth

Observances on the Sunday nearest July 6 recall the martyrdom of John Hus at the Council of Constance in 1415. The All Saints liturgy (page 105 in the *Book of Worship*) is appropriate on this day with the liturgist thanking the Lord for calling John Hus "to be an instrument of reformation and renewal in your church, and for keeping him faithful even unto a martyr's death." In addition, hymn 391 has a verse devoted to the remembrance of John Hus.

Since July 6 falls so near the Fourth of July many churches in America either combine or substitute Independence Day observances for the martyrdom of John Hus. The National Occasions liturgy (page 139) is often used in this manner.

August Thirteenth

Following May 12, 1727, when the residents of Herrnhut agreed to live together in brotherly accord, they held many conferences and many prayer meetings. Finally they felt that they were ready to unite in a celebration of the Lord's Supper, and it was held on Wednesday morning, August 13, 1727, in the parish church at Berthelsdorf. This Lutheran church was also on the estate of Count Zinzendorf and was about one mile from the village of Herrnhut.

As the service began two young women were confirmed for their first participation in the Lord's Supper. Count Zinzendorf offered an impassioned prayer. So great was the blessing felt during this communion and so great and lasting was its influence that it has been called the birthday of the renewed Unitas Fratrum, or Moravian Church. The anniversary is one of the greatest and most important festivals of the Moravian Church.

Probably for the centennial of the event, the English Moravian poet, James Montgomery, wrote the best word-picture known of what took place on August 13, 1727, and its results:

They walked with God in peace and love
　　But failed with one another;
While sternly for the faith they strove
　　Brother fell out with brother.
But He in whom they put their trust,
Who knew their frames that they were dust,
　　Pitied and healed their weakness.

He found them in His house of prayer
With one accord assembled,
And so revealed His presence there
They wept for joy and trembled.
One cup they drank, one bread they brake,
One baptism shared, one language spake,
Forgiving and forgiven.

Then forth they went, with tongues of flame
In one blest theme delighting;
The love of Jesus, and His Name,
God's children all uniting.
That love our theme and watchword still;
That law of love may we fulfill
And love as we are loved.

The hymn, slightly altered, appears in the 1995 *Book of Worship*, 396.

August Seventeenth

Children generally follow the example of their parents, whether for good or evil, and the children had not been forgotten in the spiritual movement in Herrnhut in 1727. Quite naturally, therefore, the blessing of August Thirteenth, poured out upon the adult congregation, was followed in a few days by an awakening among the children. A personal assurance of her own salvation came to young Susanna Kuehnel, and since her home stood next to the orphanage school, her testimony of her experience quickly spread, first among other little girls and then among little boys. It culminated on August 17, a date still observed in some congregations as the Children's Festival.

The practice of encouraging religious expression by young people was common in early Herrnhut and continues today as a strong emphasis of the Moravian Church. Many congregations hold services specifically for children; teenagers may lead a Sunday morning service on a "Youth Sunday;" in some congregations the Boards of Elders and Trustees may include a specifically elected youth representative; and provincial and interprovincial youth synods are periodically held.

September Sixteenth

On September 16, 1741, a "synodical conference" of the Moravian Church was in session in London, England. It consisted of 10 persons, including Count Zinzendorf, his wife Erdmuth Dorothea, their 16-year-old daughter Benigna, Leonard Dober, and August Gottlieb Spangenberg and his wife, Maria.

The meeting had been called to consider the administration of affairs during Zinzendorf's approaching visit to America. Decisions, however, were complicated by Leonard Dober's declining to continue in the office of Chief Elder.

It is not surprising that Dober found the load too heavy to bear. When he was solemnly installed at Herrnhut in 1735 the Unitas Fratrum was small and not widely scattered, but it had grown rapidly in six years, and the responsibility of the Chief Elder — essentially shepherding all the spiritual matters of the Unity — had increased accordingly.

Dober had filled the office worthily, supported by the Lord, but finally it grew too much for him, and he asked for release. Then the synodical conference tried to find someone who had the necessary qualifications and who also had the love and confidence of all the congregations. Several were suggested, but not one received unanimous support from members of the conference.

Finally the question was asked, "Would not the Lord our Savior be so gracious as to accept this office for Himself? To Him alone no objection could be raised." All members of the conference agreed that this would solve their problem, and all "accepted Him with joy and deep humility." Dober's resignation was accepted, and his pastoral duties were divided among several others, while he retained supervision of mission activities. A "General Conference" assumed Zinzendorf's administrative work.

This idea of the headship of Christ in the Church on earth was sound and scriptural, and the conception of this headship, as a supreme pastoral relation of the Chief Shepherd to His flock, which He had purchased with His own blood, had its warrant in numerous utterances of Christ and His Apostles.

By this experience the Moravian Church was saved from a spiritual hierarchy. It continued to function under the Scripture which gave it the name Unitas Fratrum: One is your Master, even Christ; and all ye are brethren (Matt. 23:8, KJV). It carried with it the Moravian conception of the ministry, namely, that ministers are absolutely the property of Christ, unreservedly consecrated to His service.

September 16 is therefore observed as the covenant day of ministers and church workers of the Moravian Church.

November Thirteenth

The synodical conference which met in London that September 16, 1741, had had the wonderful experience of the definite realization that the Lord Jesus Christ, by His own word, was Master, Head, Chief Elder of His Brethren's Church. The conference knew, though, the length of time required to send a message to distant points. It therefore appointed November 13 as the day on which simultaneous announcement should be made to all Moravian congregations of the events of September 16.

In the Moravian congregations of Europe the news was received with proud emotion and humble joy. American Moravians did not hear what had happened until too late for that November 13, but on November 13, 1742, the congregation of

Bethlehem observed its anniversary, with Count Zinzendorf in their midst to tell them all about it.

The anniversary of this announcement to the congregations has become one of the great festivals of the Moravian Church.

The purpose of celebrating the historical event with special services, lovefeasts, and the holy communion is to offer to every member the opportunity to realize that Jesus Christ is the Head and Chief Elder of the Church. He is also the Head of each individual believer, and on this day members should consciously renew their pledge of loyalty and confirm in the sacrament of the Lord's Supper their personal fellowship with their Savior.

Lovefeasts

The holding of lovefeasts, after the practice of the Apostolic Church, has come to be one of the outstanding customs of the Moravian Church and has proved to be a real means of grace. Members of other denominations are attracted to Moravian lovefeasts in large numbers, and thus the spirit of fellowship is greatly advanced.

Lovefeasts originated in the first gathering of Christians after Pentecost. The early believers met and broke bread together, thereby signifying their union and equality. These meals of the church family were associated with the celebration of the Lord's Supper, which followed them. They were called *agape*, from the Greek word for love, that is for the highest type of spiritual love. Gradually the *agape* lost its devotional character, and toward the end of the fourth century the Church gave it up.

The lovefeast of Apostolic times was resuscitated in its original simplicity by the Moravian Church in 1727. After the memorable celebration of the holy communion on August 13, seven groups of the participants continued to talk over the great spiritual blessing which they had experienced and were reluctant to separate and return to their own homes for the noonday meal. Count Zinzendorf, sensing the situation, sent them food from his manor house, and each group partook together, continuing in prayer, religious conversation, and the singing of hymns. This incident reminded Zinzendorf of the primitive *agape*, and the idea was fostered until lovefeasts became a custom in Moravian life. They were introduced wherever new settlements were founded and so came to America.

Wherever its fullest liturgical development exists, the lovefeast is a service of solemn dignity, in which the finest Moravian Church hymns and stately music may be heard, but without any surrender of its central idea.

Because of its attraction for visitors, persons sometimes come to a lovefeast out of curiosity, perhaps amused at the idea of "eating in church." It is interesting to see such a person yield to the spirit of devotion which pervades the service and change in a very few moments from visitor to reverent member of the service. This never fails when the congregation is itself full of the spirit of reverence and Christian love.

The lovefeast is primarily a song service, opened with prayer. Often there is no address; the hymns in the ode, or order of service, furnish the subject matter for devotional thoughts. If many visitors are present, the presiding minister often says a few words, explaining the purpose of the service, just before the congregation partakes of the bun and coffee, or whatever is served. On special occasions an address may be added, giving opportunity to remind the congregation of the history of the anniversary or the deeper import of the day.

There is no rule as to the food to be offered, except that it be very simple and easily distributed. The drink may be coffee, tea, or lemonade, fully prepared in advance, so that it may be served very quietly and without interruption of the singing. Usually mugs are used, which may be passed from hand to hand along a pew from a tray brought along the aisle. A slightly sweetened bun, which can be served in baskets passed along the pews, is a convenient form of bread. Usually men handle the trays of mugs, and women the baskets of buns. While the congregation partakes, the choir sings an anthem. Later the mugs are quietly gathered and removed. The food served is not consecrated, as in the communion. Children and members of any denomination may partake.

There are many services during the year at which a lovefeast is appropriate, such as the festivals of the church year, the anniversary days of the Moravian Church, the anniversary day of a congregation, a missionary occasion, any day in fact on which there is a desire to stress the headship of the Lord and the oneness and fellowship of His followers.

New Year's Eve

In early days when news traveled slowly some Moravian churches made special use of New Year's Eve to review the events of the year, particularly from the standpoint of the Church.

From the diaries and other records kept during the year the minister of such a congregation would prepare the "Memorabilia," or annual summary of important items in the life of the congregation. This historical sketch was read to the congregation and then was placed on file in the archives. Over the years these Memorabilia have become of great value to historians.

The schedule of services on New Year's Eve varies in different congregations from lovefeasts to Watchnight services. In the Watchnight service there is prayer, hymns are sung, and a minister makes a short address. The signal for the changing year is given by the organ or by the band which leads the congregation in singing the traditional hymn,

> *Now thank we all our God*
> *With heart and hands and voices.*

The *Texts* of the first day of January are read; prayer is offered for the guidance of God during the new year; and after another hymn the service closes with the benediction.

Daily Texts

With the opening of each new year many Moravian families begin reading the new edition of the *Moravian Daily Texts,* or *Daily Texts* as it is familiarly called, or *Text Book.*

The Moravian Church was a pioneer in the publication of a book for use in public and private daily devotions. Even today in many countries in Europe the *Daily Texts* is the only such devotional book available.

Once again, this custom can be traced to Herrnhut and to Count Zinzendorf. He usually held the evening devotionals, and during the service on May 3, 1728, he read a "watchword" from Scripture for the people to remember and think about during the following day. As the congregation grew and not all members were able to attend the evening service, someone was appointed to go to each home in the morning and announce the text for the day.

So long as he lived Count Zinzendorf arranged the texts, drawing them from a large collection which he gradually assembled from the Bible. In 1730 he chose in advance the texts for 1731, and they were printed in the first *Text Book.* This method of advance preparation has been followed ever since, except that after the death of Zinzendorf the texts were arranged by a committee instead of an individual.

From the age-old collection of texts certain leading ministers of the Moravian Church in Herrnhut, Germany, draw a watchword for each day of the approaching year, prayer being offered that each may be a message from God to His people. An appropriate doctrinal text from the New

Testament is then selected to accompany each watchword. These texts are then sent to each province of the Unity and are translated into the language of the people. In many places a few lines from some hymn are added to each text to emphasize or explain the thought.

Each province is at liberty to include in its *Daily Texts* such additional material as it considers desirable. The North American edition publishes the appropriate Scripture texts from the three-year lectionary — Old Testament, Psalm, Epistle, and Gospel — for each Sunday. For other days of the week Scripture passages are suggested for devotional reading. Also included in the North American edition is a prayer for each day and historical notes of such things of interest as anniversaries of congregations and memorial days of the Church.

Worldwide the *Daily Texts* is printed in 51 languages and dialects, from Czech to Tibetan, Zulu to Inuktut (Labrador). The number of readers cannot be stated even approximately, but it is widely used by members of other denominations as well as by Moravians. The good which it has done over 275 years can never be estimated.

Many incidents in ancient records, family tradition, and modern experience, testify to the remarkable way in which these texts fit into the daily life of their readers. One incident, recently discovered in a Unity diary of 1751, may be given as an example. The missionaries Mack and Froelick were passing through a Pennsylvania forest when they were alarmed by the discovery that Indians had set the woods on fire and flames were all around them. The only chance for escape seemed to be directly forward through a narrow passage where the sides were already burning. They reached safety with only some slight singeing of hair and clothing. The text for that day of deliverance was, "When you walk through fire you shall not be burned, and the flame shall not consume you" (Isa. 43:2).

The same text would apply to the cherished collection of texts from which the watchwords are drawn, for it came uninjured through the flames which swept Herrnhut on the last day of World War II.

chapter V

A CHURCH FAMILY

The Choir System

Among the surprisingly modern ideas developed by the Moravian Church in the middle of the 18th century was the Choir system.

The word choir comes from a Greek word meaning group, and with that meaning there is still a choir of singers in most churches.

With a very modern realization of the value of group interests and group activities, the Moravians divided their congregations into Choirs or groups, the groups naturally drawn together by sex, age, and condition. In its fullest development each congregation had its group of widowers, of widows, of married people, single men, single women, older boys, older girls, little boys, and little girls. The adult groups were organized with appropriate officers, and often with group funds. Frequently the Choirs had houses, known as the Brothers House, the Sisters House, or the Widows House, where members of the group lived and carried on the usual activities of life.

For each group there were meetings, appropriate to the age and interests of the group. Of special note were the Choir festivals or covenant days held annually, usually on a date of historic interest. These were days of prayer and renewed dedication to the service of Christ.

The first Choir or group to organize was led by Anna Nitschmann. On May 4, 1730, she and other young women of Herrnhut entered into a covenant to dedicate their lives wholly to the service of the Lord in whatever field they might be called, whether as Single Sisters or as married, whether in the home or in foreign lands. The covenant day of the Single Sisters is therefore May 4.

For the Married People's Choir the day chosen for the annual covenant day was September 7. This was selected as a compliment to Count and Countess Zinzendorf, who were married on September 7, 1722.

The covenant day of the Single Brethren comes on August 29, the anniversary of the day in 1741 when the young men of Herrnhut organized for Christian service along their own lines.

Originally the Widowers had their own Choir and their own covenant day, August 31. In America, where widowers were always few in number, they sometimes joined with the Single Brethren and sometimes with the Married People, ultimately choosing the latter group.

The Widows maintained a separate organization for a much longer time with April 30 as their covenant day, but they finally merged with the Married People in their covenant day. In the same way the Older Boys (July 9) joined the Single Brethren; and the Older Girls (June 4) joined the Single Sisters.

August 17 became the special day for Little Girls following the religious experiences of Susanna Kuehnel and other children in 1727. For a number of years the festival for the Little Boys was observed on June 24, but later it was transferred to August 17, which has since been known as the Children's Festival.

Over the years the Choir system was laid aside in many Moravian churches, and today is practiced only in the graveyard, God's Acre, where individuals are still buried with their Choir.

Marriage

The Moravian Church considers marriage to be a "holy relationship," and "not to be entered into unadvisedly or lightly, but discreetly, thoughtfully, and with reverence for God."

As early as 1764 a special marriage liturgy was prepared for use at Moravian weddings. In response to the solemn questions of the marriage ceremony (*Book of Worship*, pp. 175-6) the man and woman pledge themselves "to live together in the holy bond of marriage," and to be "faithful Christian husband and wife so long as both shall live."

A Moravian member is not forbidden to marry a member of another church, but young people are urged to choose Christian partners for their journey through life and to abide faithfully by their marriage vows. If the bride is a Moravian, her own pastor should perform the ceremony.

Moravian Dress

The so-called Moravian costumes used today for pageants or other occasions, where something distinctive is desired, are merely copies of portraits in the Moravian Archives in Bethlehem, Pennsylvania.

Old prints of services in Herrnhut show a uniformity of dress, but this seems to have been limited to a few congregations. Portraits of leaders of the European Moravian Church in the 18th century show quite a variety of styles. Except for the use of the surplice on sacramental occasions, Moravian ministers wore no vestments, but dressed like other men of their period.

The old minute books indicate that in America there was no rule governing the dress of men or women, except that simplicity was stressed. Members were urged to live within their means, and extravagance was deplored. Being fashionable met with disfavor, because that was considered "an improper attempt to attract attention." In general, the clothes of men and women were the more simple types of their day, except that the women for church services wore the Haube, a white linen cap with the ribbon color indicating the Choir to which they belonged, generally red for Older Girls, pink for Single Sisters, blue for Married Sisters, or white for Widows.

Today, North American Moravians dress like their contemporaries.

Funerals

A distinctive feature of a Moravian funeral is its simplicity. The *Book of Worship* provides a liturgy titled "Memorial Service and Burial," the first part for use in the service in the church, the second part at the grave. This liturgy is primarily a compilation of passages from the Bible that emphasize praise to God and a firm belief in the Resurrection and life eternal. The keynote is sounded in the words, "Living Redeemer, we find our hope in you."

Other features of a Moravian funeral are readings from the Scriptures, prayers, and the singing of hymns. Congregational singing of the great hymns of the Church is usually a part of our funerals. Indeed music is one of the two features that are unique to the Moravian Church in its practices associated with the burial of the dead.

The use of a band at the graveside service is a common practice, particularly in congregations that have their own God's Acre. The band is customarily stationed near the grave awaiting the arrival of the funeral procession. As the procession moves toward the grave the band plays a chorale such as "Goudimel" (205 A). During the concluding part of the liturgy, which comprises the entire service at the grave, the band accompanies as the congregation sings two hymn stanzas. One is the committal hymn (Tune 14 A),

Now to the earth let these remains
In hope committed be,
Until the body changed attains
Blest immortality.

The other is the closing stanza (Tune 22 A),

The Saviour's blood and righteousness
My beauty is, my glorious dress;
Thus well arrayed I need not fear,
When in His presence I appear.

After the benediction the band plays as a postlude a chorale such as, "Lord, for Thy Coming Us Prepare" (79 A), often followed by, "Tis the Most Blest and Needful Part" (159 A). If the deceased was a minister or served in the musical life of the Church such as the band or choir, the band may play after chorale 79 A the "Requiem" (tune 602 A), which is associated with the words,

Sleep thy last sleep,
Free from care and sorrow;
Rest, where none weep,
Till the eternal morrow;
Though dark waves roll
O'er the silent river,
Thy fainting soul
Jesus can deliver.

A second unique feature of a Moravian funeral is the reading of a memoir of the departed member. The memoir is a brief biography of the deceased prepared by the pastor. These memoirs are deposited in the archives of the province and afford a store of valuable genealogical information in later years.

The custom of burial in God's Acre according to the Choir system rather than in family groups emphasizes the nature of the Church as the family of God.

The Moravian Covenant for Christian Living

When descendants of the ancient Unitas Fratrum settled Herrnhut in 1722 they were soon joined by other people with differing backgrounds and ideals. To put an end to the resulting confusion many conferences were held, and on May 12, 1727, the men and women of Herrnhut met with Count Zinzendorf to consider statutes which had been drawn up for the regulation of life in the community. After the Count had explained every article in detail, he invited those who wished to subscribe to come forward and give him their hands, and every man and woman present complied.

This *Brotherly Agreement*, as it was called, meant much to the residents in Herrnhut. From a restless, separated, uncertain people they became so united in a common purpose that it attracted the attention of the world of their day and brought many new members into their group.

Since 1727 the *Brotherly Agreement*, or *Moravian Covenant for Christian Living* as it is called today, has been revised a number of times to bring it into conformity with the best thought of members of congregations in different parts of the world in the change of conditions that always come with the years.

The *Moravian Covenant for Christian Living* is neither a creed nor a doctrinal thesis. It sets a pattern for Christian living, a practical standard for the life of church members in everyday affairs, as well as in relation to the Church.

The Cup of Covenant

The Cup of Covenant, or Cup of Thanksgiving, was used for the first time in Herrnhut in 1728 to "prepare the heart for the communion which could not be held just then."

During the earlier years of the renewed Unitas Fratrum, or Moravian Church, it was used frequently "to give thanks for special manifestations of grace and to covenant together for new faithfulness in the service of Jesus." In Salem, North Carolina, the school teachers and other leaders among the young people and children met annually to discuss their duties, receive the thanks of the congregation for their labors, and to share the Cup of Covenant as they pledged themselves to renewed fidelity and zeal in their work.

This Cup of Thanksgiving was based on the first cup in the Passover meal (Luke 22:17) and is not to be confused with the second cup (Luke 22:20) which followed the meal and was used by the Lord in instituting the Lord's Supper.

In the North American Moravian Church the Cup of Thanksgiving, otherwise called the Cup of Covenant, is seldom used now except in connection with the covenant day of the ministers of the Moravian Church, which is observed on September 16.

The Hourly Intercession and the Table Blessing

The residents of Herrnhut had just experienced the outpouring of the Holy Spirit upon them on August 13, 1727, when two weeks later, on August 27, they began a custom that, following only a brief lapse in the 19th century, has become a central feature of the Moravian Church today.

This is the Hourly Intercession, where members of the congregation keep unceasing prayer to the Lord.

The first Hourly Intercession lasted for more than 100 years. It was resuscitated by the British Province on August 27, 1872, as the Moravian Prayer Union, and the General Synod of 1957 endorsed it as a practice of the worldwide Moravian Church. Today the Unity Prayer Watch, as it is called, is shared by each province in its turn. In North America, the Southern Province is assigned the month of January, the Alaska Province prays April 1-7, and the Northern

Province's turn is November 16-December 31.

Another prayer practice among Moravians is the table grace or blessing at mealtimes, thanking the Lord for the bounties bestowed upon us. A favorite among Moravians is a simple prayer: "Come, Lord Jesus, our guest to be, and bless these gifts bestowed by thee." It was a popular table blessing in Germany in the 1700's, and it appears as early as our 1783 German Moravian hymnal. A second verse, though not strictly a table grace, has become popular in recent years: "Bless thy dear ones everywhere, and keep them in thy loving care."

Sunday Schools

The Moravian Church was rather slow to organize Sunday schools.

In 1780 an Anglican layman named Robert Raikes established a Sunday school at Gloucester, England. Into his school he gathered poor, uneducated boys and taught them to read, especially to read the Bible. This type of Sunday school lasted at various places until public schools became generally established.

Moravian children did not need this kind of a school. In their day schools they were taught to read, and in regular periods of religious instruction they were well grounded in the doctrines of the Christian faith.

In the first quarter of the 19th century Moravians became interested in opening the Raikes type of Sunday school for underprivileged children. Bethlehem commenced such a school in the spring of 1816; Salem followed with a school at Hopewell that September. It was 1819 before a Sunday school along more modern lines was commenced for children of the Friedland congregation, and it wasn't until 1849 that Salem opened a Sunday school for its own children.

Today the Moravian Church considers Sunday school an

important feature of congregational life as other opportunities for religious instruction of children have been curtailed. To meet this need, the Synods of both Northern and Southern Provinces elected Boards of Christian Education whose responsibility was to promote leadership education, vacation Bible schools, summer camps and conferences, catechetical instruction, and to provide approved curriculum materials for the Sunday schools.

The two provinces also organized an Interprovincial Board of Christian Education, which has evolved into the Interprovincial Board of Communication (IBOC) and is responsible for the publication of Moravian books and literature and oversees the publishing of *The Moravian*, the Church's monthly magazine. The IBOC is responsibile for publishing resources (including this booklet) and producing the North American version of the *Daily Texts* in accordance with its purpose and mission which states:

"The purpose of the Interprovincial Board of Communication (IBOC) is to promote the image, ministry, heritage, doctrine, life, and mission of the Moravian Church; to provide information about its activities and opportunities; and to inspire and equip individuals within the Moravian Church and beyond to grow in their personal relationship with Jesus Christ and to serve as his disciples. The board shall provide resources in print, audio-visual, and electronic media to make this possible. It shall carry out its own goals and assignments and work in cooperation with the other arms of the denomination."